Inside these pages you will find the tools you need to develop your reflective writing.

I have divided the book into three sections.

- *The first section introduces you to key theories of critically reflective practice, showing how you can use these to gain greater self-awareness and develop your work. Space for writing is provided to help you get started.*
- *The second section is designed to support you in writing more freely. Quotations, structured activities and helpful prompts encourage you to write at a deeper level.*
- *The final section explores 'where next?' and is designed to help you see what could be on the horizon.*

A number of my own students who have studied critically reflective practice have said, 'I knew I would learn a lot on my course, but I didn't realise how much I would learn about myself.'

I hope you will find this journal just as useful.

Signed

Barbara Bassot

Canterbury Christ Church University, UK.

'Reflective journal writing must be one of the most valuable development activities professionals can engage in. And yet most do not because they do not know how. Bassot's straightforward account, with its clear study of many approaches and strategies to try, will put them on the right path.' – *Dr Gillie Bolton*, author of *Reflective Practice Writing 4e*

'In *The Reflective Journal* Barbara Bassot has created a very useful and flexible tool. The combination of theory and experiential opportunity will allow both the novice and the experienced reflective writer to learn, deepen and develop their practice. Many of the techniques and exercises will continue to be of benefit long after the empty pages here have been filled.' – *Kate Thompson MA*, author of *Therapeutic Journal Writing: An Introduction for Professionals*

'I welcome this immensely practical approach to enabling students to develop their skills and understanding of writing reflectively. It is packed full of useful exercises which encourage the reader to try techniques and explore approaches. The focus on one idea at a time is an excellent way to encourage students to get to grips with an essential technique for professional practice.' – *Melanie Jasper*, *Professor of Nursing, Head of College of Human and Health Sciences, Swansea University, UK*

'*The Reflective Journal* takes the reader on a systematic journey to becoming a critically reflective practitioner. Using an innovative format, with interesting insights presented through quotes, this visually stimulating journal will be helpful to not only students on professional programmes, but also practitioners in their reflective practice.' – *Divya Jindal-Snape*, *Professor in Education, Inclusion and Life Transitions, University of Dundee, UK*

The Reflective Journal

Barbara Bassot

palgrave
macmillan

First published 2013 by
PALGRAVE MACMILLAN

Palgrave Macmillan in the UK is an imprint of Macmillan Publishers Limited, registered in England, company number 785998, of Houndmills, Basingstoke, Hampshire RG21 6XS.

Palgrave Macmillan in the US is a division of St Martin's Press LLC, 175 Fifth Avenue, New York, NY 10010.

Palgrave Macmillan is the global academic imprint of the above companies and has companies and representatives throughout the world.

Palgrave® and Macmillan® are registered trademarks in the United States, the United Kingdom, Europe and other countries

ISBN: 9781–137–32471–9

This book is printed on paper suitable for recycling and made from fully managed and sustained forest sources. Logging, pulping and manufacturing processes are expected to conform to the environmental regulations of the country of origin.

A catalogue record for this book is available from the British Library.
A catalog record for this book is available from the Library of Congress.

Printed in China

Contents

Acknowledgements

The author and publisher would like to thank the following publishers and organisations for permission to reproduce copyright material:

Anne Riches for extracts on page 54 from A. Riches: *'Where did that come from?' How to Keep Control in any Situation* (2012: 9–24). Ed Muzio for Figure 5 on page 68 from http://www.groupharmonics. com/HelpDesk/Ladder.htm (2011). Institute of Career Guidance for Figure 8 on page 162 from B. Bassot 'Career learning and development: A bridge to the future, in H. Reid (ed.) *Constructing the Future: Career Guidance for Changing Contexts* (2009: 4). McGraw Hill for Figure 2 on page 48 from H. Luft: *Group Processes: An Introduction to Group Dynamics* (1984: 60). Nelson Thornes Ltd for the extract on page 25 from M. Jasper: *Beginning Reflective Practice* (2003: 197–8). Nova Science Publishers Inc. for the extracts on pages 141 and 145 from H. L. Reid and B. Bassot: 'Reflection: A constructive space for career development', in M. McMahon and M. Watson (eds) *Career Counselling and Constructivism: Elaboration of constructs* (2011: 107). Oxford Centre for Staff and Learning Development, Oxford Brookes University for Figure 3 on page 58 from http://www. brookes.ac.uk/services/upgrade/study-skills/reflective-gibbs.html. Pearson TalentLens for the extract on page 11 from 'The Learning Styles Questionnaire' from http://www.peterhoney.com/ content/LearningStylesQuestionnaire.html. RoutledgeFalmer for the extracts on pages 39 and 61 from D. Boud, R. Keogh and D. Walker: *Reflection: Turning Experience into Learning* (1985: 19); and M. Eraut: *Developing Professional Knowledge and Competence* (1994: 28). Routledge David Fulton Press for the extracts on pages 71 and 91 from T. Ghaye and K. Ghaye: *Teaching and Learning through Critical Reflective Practice* (1998: 16, 19). Routledge for the extract on page 81 from T. Ghaye: *Teaching and Learning through Reflective Practice*, 2nd edition (2011: 20). Sage Learning Matters for the extract on page 15 from L. Howatson-Jones: *Reflective Practice in Nursing* (2010: 120); for the extract on page 85 from A. Campbell and L. Norton: *Learning Teaching and Assessing in Higher Education* (2007: 141); for the extract on page 113 from C. Knott and T. Scragg: *Reflective Practice in Social Work*, 2nd edition (2010: 6). Sage Publication Inc for the extracts on pages 7, 27 and 133, from K. F. Osterman and R. B Kottkamp: *Reflective Practice for Educators,* 2nd edition (2004: 23, 24, 32). Sage Publication Ltd for the extract on page 95 from G. Bolton: *Reflective Practice: Writing and Professional Development*, 2nd edition (2005: 24). Pearson Education, Inc, for Figure 1 on page 26 from D. A. Kolb: *Experiential Learning: Experience as the Source of Learning & Development* (1984: 21); for the extract on page 57 from C. Johns: *Guided Reflection: a Narrative Approach to Advancing Professional Practice* (2010: 37); for the extracts on pages 101 and 137 from C. Johns: *Becoming a Reflective Practitioner*, 2nd edition (2004: 5, 6); for the extract on page 117 from C. Johns: *Becoming a Reflective Practitioner* 3rd edition (2009: xi); for the extract on page 37 from D. A. Schön: *Educating the Reflective Practitioner* (1987: 26); for the extracts on pages 65 and 121 from S. D. Brookfield: *Becoming a Critically Reflective Teacher* (1995: xii, 2); for the extract on page 75 from C. Bulman and S. Schutz: *Reflective Practice in Nursing*, 4th edition (2008: 7).

Introduction

Welcome to *The Reflective Journal*. Whether you are a student on a professional course in a university or college, someone undertaking a work-based qualification, or a professional practitioner who wants to continue to develop their knowledge and skills, *The Reflective Journal* is designed to help you to reflect on your practice and thereby enhance your personal and professional development.

The aims of *The Reflective Journal* are fourfold. First, it takes you on a journey from reflective practice to critically reflective practice. Reflective practice encourages us to review our learning experiences, whilst critically reflective practice means that we begin to engage with our emotional responses and to challenge some of the assumptions we might be making about people and situations. It also asks us to consider issues of power, for example in relationships and organisations.

Second, *The Reflective Journal* introduces you to a broad range of theoretical models of reflection. These models are often abstract and thereby difficult to apply in practice. Some would even argue that knowledge of such theory does not help you reflect. However, Thompson (1995: 29) rightly cautions us against 'the fallacy of theoryless practice' and the practice of reflection is no exception to this. Having an understanding of these theoretical models will help you to reflect at a deeper level by highlighting things that might not be obvious on the surface. This journal serves as a tool to help you build a deeper knowledge of reflective practice by applying theories of reflection to your ongoing learning and development.

Third, the journal enables you to record your learning and development, so that you can return to it in the future. Many of us think that we will remember things that happen in our lives, particularly things that we feel are significant at the time. But in reality, especially when our day-to-day lives are so busy, we can forget even those things that we were convinced at the time we would remember.

The fourth aim of *The Reflective Journal* is to enable you to gain a deeper understanding of yourself and your practice through writing. At a writers' seminar I once attended, the leader of the session said, 'I have to write about things in order to understand them.' At the time, this was something of a revelation to me, as I always thought that people (like him) who wrote a lot did so because they already understood a lot. The process of writing forces us to slow down and to take time to reflect, which allows our knowledge and understandings to grow. Unlike many of the books you will read, this is one that you will be able to write in – and I encourage you to do so!

No doubt you are currently entering a time when you will gain lots of useful knowledge and skills in relation to your professional development. Through this learning process you will also find that some of your attitudes and the way you think about things will be challenged.

'I always knew I would learn a lot, but I never realised how much I would learn about myself.'

Many professional practitioners are aware of the value of reflection in their day-to-day work and most professional courses include modules on reflective practice and professional development. Students on professional courses are often asked to keep a reflective diary or journal and *The Reflective Journal* will help you as you study these particular modules and also on your course as a whole.

How to use this journal

The Reflective Journal is designed as a tool to help you reflect, thereby enabling you to take a deep approach to your learning and development. When asked to keep a reflective diary or journal by their tutors, many do not find this easy. *The Reflective Journal* shows you how to start writing reflectively and how to develop your writing to enable critical reflection.

Part 1 is broken down into ten themes. Each theme starts with a brief introduction and is followed by four pieces of content based on the theme where some key theories are introduced in an accessible way. These are followed by a number of blank spaces for your written reflections, including some practical activities to help you to apply theory to your practice. The quotes provided are included for close reading – by examining each word and phrase in detail you can gain a deeper understanding of yourself and your practice.

The theory discussed in *The Reflective Journal* is drawn from a range of academic disciplines, such as health and social care, education, counselling, business and management. Throughout, the word client is often used to refer to the people who you will engage with in your capacity as a professional. If this is not an appropriate term for your particular context, please use an alternative, such as patient or student. You will also find a number of quotes from students interspersed amongst the text. These serve as examples of reflective writing and could act as a source of inspiration.

Part 2 contains further activities and quotes, along with more blank pages for reflective writing. These serve as further prompts for thinking critically about your practice.

Part 3 focuses on CV building and career development. This section contains activities to help you think about your experience more broadly, particularly in relation to how your professional knowledge and skills are developing. It can also serve as a helpful record for the future.

The Reflective Journal introduces you to a wide range of relevant theory. In this particular respect, it should be seen only as a good starting point; it is very likely that you will want to read more. At the back of the journal, there are examples of further reading highlighting some of the texts on reflective practice that you might find useful; there are many more and you should always use the reading lists provided by your tutors. In addition, there is a full list of references in the Harvard style and an index of some of the key terms used.

Most people who are new to reflective writing need to know where and how to start. Perhaps most importantly, they need to be assured that their writing is reflective and not merely descriptive. A good place to start is by reading the journal's list of contents and then completing the first two themes. This should help you to begin to start writing reflectively. The journal is written to enable you to think at an increasingly deeper level as you work your way through it. However, you should not feel that you have to follow the order of the themes rigidly, particularly if certain topics and theories are being covered in your lectures or seminars. You should feel free to use it as best suits you. It is important to be aware that there is a danger in using the journal mechanically, for example by writing a specific amount each week or feeling that you cannot look ahead. This could mean that writing becomes a chore that you gain little from.

Many people find that the time they spend writing reflectively is time well invested. I hope that you find *The Reflective Journal* helpful in your learning and professional development.

I would like to express my sincere thanks to my family and friends for their tireless support in the process of bringing *The Reflective Journal* to fruition. In particular, I would like to thank Phil Bassot for his careful work on the diagrams, Marc Bassot for his excellent proof reading and constructive comments, and Morag Greenwood for her impeccable work in obtaining the relevant permissions. My grateful thanks also to all the students who gave me permission to include their quotes, which have inspired me and I am sure will inspire others. Finally, I would like to thank my Commissioning Editor, Catherine Gray, for her belief in the project and the publisher for being prepared to take a risk with a new kind of publication.

Barbara Bassot

Part 1

Models and tools for reflection

Beginnings

This section will:

- Help you begin to understand the process of transition and what often happens when you start something new
- Introduce you to the concept of the 'metaphorical mirror'
- Emphasise the importance of having a personal vision
- Help you begin to examine your learning styles

Theme 1.1 Starting something new

Beginning something new in our lives is almost always challenging; it can be both exciting and daunting at the same time, even when it is something you have been looking forward to. If you are starting something new at the moment you have begun a process of transition.

Various words come to mind to describe a transition and some are as follows:

- Exciting
- New
- Different
- Scary
- Taxing
- Emotional

You may be able to think of others. During your process of transition you may feel or experience some, or even all of them.

It is common to experience a range of different feelings as you progress through the transition process. In their seminal work, Adams, Hayes and Hopson (1976) describe how many people think and feel during the following seven stages of the transition process.

1 **Immobilisation** – the process is new and we have a feeling of being overwhelmed by the enormity of what is happening. This means we could 'freeze'.

2 **Reaction of elation or despair** – if the transition is seen as positive, we have feelings of elation, if negative we have a sense of despair.

3 **Self-doubt or minimisation** – as the transition becomes more real, our elation turns to self-doubt and as our feelings dip, questions arise such as 'can I actually do this?' Alternatively feelings of despair turn to minimisation, for example 'maybe this won't be so bad after all'.

4 **Acceptance and letting go** – as we accept that the change is happening, our thoughts begin to turn to the future and we start to let go of the past.

5 **Testing** – as we get used to the new situation, we begin to try out new ways of working and living.

6 **Search for meaning** – a period when we spend time reflecting on what has happened in order to explore what the change means for us.

7 **Integration** – the meaning is internalised and change is accepted into our everyday lives.

It is helpful to understand that these stages of transition show us that people often experience highs and lows over a period of time as they experience change.

Try this   Describe your recent experiences of transition. Have you experienced any of Adams et al.'s (1976) stages? If so, which ones stand out in your memory? Are there any that do not seem appropriate to your situation? There is a space below for you to use, if you want to.

The 'metaphorical mirror'

When looking in a concise dictionary for the word 'reflection', you will find at least two different definitions – a mirror image and thinking. Over time you will develop, through a process of thinking and looking at your practice in a 'metaphorical mirror'. This will heighten your levels of critical evaluation and self-awareness, as you examine your knowledge, skills and attitudes. Many of us look into different types of mirrors each day – here are some examples that give us insights into reflective practice:

- **The bathroom mirror** – most of us will get up in the morning and look in the bathroom mirror. We then make a choice; we can decide to leave things as they are or take some action to make ourselves more presentable to the outside world! Examining our practice means that we are not always happy with what we find. However, taking action or not always involves choice.

> *'This word "reflection" – I never thought it would be so interesting.'*

- **The driver's mirror** – this is a vital tool that people use every time they get into the driver's seat. By using it we can see what is behind us and assess whether or not it is safe to move ahead. Reflective practice means looking back on experiences we have had, so that we know how to move forward.

- **Wing mirrors** – these also help us to see what is behind us when driving. Most wing mirrors also have a small mirror included within them that helps us to see what is just over our shoulder, or in a blind spot. Feedback from others plays a vital part in helping us to identify what might be a blind spot in our practice.

- **The magnifying mirror** – this is indispensable in situations where we need to look at our faces closely, for example when shaving or applying make-up. The close examination of an incident can mean that we avoid mistakes in the future.

- **The funfair mirrors** – clearly we do not look in these regularly, and these mirrors distort what we see. Some practitioners always feel that what they did was fine because they did their best, while others tend to be very hard on themselves and always find fault with what they did. In both cases it is likely that there is some kind of distortion here. This points to the vital role of feedback from, and discussion with, others; this helps to get a more accurate picture of our practice (see Theme 5).

'While experience is the basis for learning, learning cannot take place without reflection.'

(Osterman and Kottkamp, 2004: 24)

Theme **1.3** 'Begin with the end in mind'

When starting something new, particularly if it involves a large commitment of time, it is important to think about what we want to achieve. In his work *The 7 Habits of Highly Effective People*, Covey (2004: 95) urges us to 'begin with the end in mind' (Habit 2). He argues that everything is created twice – first in our minds and then in the practice of our everyday lives. He emphasises the importance of having a personal vision for the future and that focusing on the end result or outcome is one way of helping us to begin to see this more clearly. Interestingly, he also argues that if we do not have our own vision, we could live lives where the vision and priorities of others become more important than our own.

It is worth spending some time thinking about what you hope to achieve in the coming months. If you have recently embarked on a course of study, what are you hoping to gain from it? Think about the following questions:

- What are your long-term goals? Whether you have a specific career goal or not, imagine you are talking to a friend five years from now, how would you like to describe what you are doing?
- What made you choose what you are doing at the moment? What do you hope to gain from it?
- Where does your sense of achievement lie?
- What are you looking forward to most?
- What are the key areas where you feel you need to develop?
- What could hinder your development?
- How could you overcome the barriers to your development?

Whatever your responses to these questions, having a clear vision can play a vital part in maintaining your motivation and commitment to your personal and professional development.

Try this Write some notes for each of the questions on the previous page. Which areas in particular do you need to work on to insure your success?

Learning styles

In order to be able to use the 'metaphorical mirror' effectively and to examine your practice in a thorough and thoughtful way, a high level of self-awareness is essential, and you can achieve this in part through self-evaluation. A vital aspect of this process is to understand more about your learning styles – this will help you to gain more from your course and to understand both your strengths and potential areas for development.

'In order to ensure my journey is a successful one, I believe that it is essential to have a good balance of all four learning styles.'

Honey and Mumford (2000) have carried out extensive work on the subject of learning styles and have identified the following four distinct styles.

- **Activists** are doers and like to be involved in new experiences. They are open-minded and enthusiastic about new ideas. They enjoy getting on with things and can achieve a lot in a short space of time
- **Reflectors** are thinkers who like to stand back and look at a situation from different perspectives. They enjoy collecting data and thinking about things carefully before coming to any conclusions. They often observe others and listen to their views before offering their own
- **Theorists** are analytical people who integrate their observations into sound theories. They think problems through in a step-by-step way. They can be perfectionists who like to fit things into a rational scheme or model. They have an ability to see things in a detached and objective way
- **Pragmatists** are practical people who are keen to try out new ideas. They prefer concepts that can be applied easily in practice. They enjoy problem solving and decision making

Most of us have a preference for more than one style. Strengths in all styles denote a strong, all round learner – so in order to gain most from your studies it is important to know your least preferred styles, as this will give you clear areas to work on as you progress.

'Learning style preferences
determine the things people learn
and the ease with which they learn
them. They exert a hidden, but powerful,
influence on learning effectiveness.'

(Honey, undated)

Try this   Think about your learning styles (Honey and Mumford, 2000). Which are your preferred styles? Which ones do you feel you need to develop?

Starting to write reflectively

This section will:

- Help you begin to understand what reflective writing is

- Enable you to understand the role of writing in reflection

    - Help you to start to write reflectively

    - Give you a structure for reflective writing

What does it mean to write reflectively?

In order to begin writing reflectively, you need to understand what reflective writing is, and equally what it is not. Here are some characteristics of reflective writing.

Reflective writing is:

- Always written in the first person (I ...) with a focus on yourself
- Generally more personal than other forms of academic writing
- Helpful when you are asked to evaluate your experiences
- Focused on your experiences, thoughts, feelings and assumptions
- A form of self-supervision
- Honest and spontaneous
- Subjective
- A record of your thoughts and experiences that you can return to
- An investment of time.

Reflective writing is not:

- Simply a description of what happened
- Written in the third person with a focus on others
- Calculated
- Objective
- Something that can be rushed
- Simply about planning what you will do next time.

Reflective writing helps us to link our ideas together and discover meanings from the things we see and experience. Our understandings become broader and deeper as we question our approaches to people and circumstances. Like any other skill, reflective writing is one that will improve with practice. Indeed reflection itself is a skill which also improves over time. As you progress, you will find that your learning will become deeper as a result of your investment of time in writing reflectively.

'Writing about your experiences will help you to make sense of them, so that your understanding lasts and contributes to your lifelong learning.'

(Howatson-Jones, 2010: 120)

The role of writing in reflection

'Writing seems to unload my mind, clear it of all those thoughts that seem to whirl around with no escape.'

When starting the process of reflective writing, it is important to understand how writing in this way can make a difference to your learning and development. Sometimes I hear people say 'but I reflect all the time, for example in the car on my way home.' It is important to emphasise that writing often leads to a significantly deeper level of reflection than thinking alone, as it slows our thought processes down. It is impossible to write about something without thinking about it at the same time – unless you are only writing something that you know already, such as a nursery rhyme that you can recite off by heart.

Brockbank and McGill (2006: 282–3) discuss the following benefits of keeping a reflective journal and describe it as 'a map of your learning journey':

- It is always available to you – it is never too busy
- It never answers back – it is always open to listen
- It maintains privacy and confidentiality
- It opens up a continuous relationship with the self
- It accepts everything and everyone unconditionally
- It does not get tired of hearing the same thing over and over again – for example 'I still find this difficult because …'
- It is written in the moment and is a true reflection of how you thought and felt at the time
- It gives you a chance to communicate with yourself
- It brings greater clarity through the process of writing
- It never disagrees with you
- It provides a record of learning and development.

You may be someone who loves journal writing and may have kept a personal journal for some time. On the other hand, you may be new to the whole idea.

No one is suggesting that writing is the only way to reflect; in fact people often find reflecting together in pairs or groups to be very helpful too (see Theme 9). However, writing has its own unique advantages.

'As a private document,
a journal can include whatever you
want it to. There are no rules about personal
reflective writing – the important thing is to use it to
achieve the purpose you are using it for, and to write in
it in a way you want to write in it.'

(Jasper, 2008: 177)

Reflective writing – how do I start?

When you have not done it before, writing a reflective journal for the first time can be difficult and many people do not know where to start. Often they ask questions such as:

- What am I meant to write?
- Where do I start?
- What if I get it all wrong?
- What if I write things that make no sense?

'I have decided to maintain this journal whether it is a masterpiece or not.'

These are natural questions to ask, and you can gain some confidence and re-assurance from Bolton's (2010: 107–18) practical advice on starting to write as part of your professional development. In her work she describes five stages of reflective writing – she calls Stage 1 'the six minute write'. Here she gives the following pointers:

- Write whatever is in your head
- Time yourself and write for six minutes without stopping
- Don't stop to examine your writing or to be critical of it; just keep writing even if it doesn't seem to make sense
- Let your writing flow; don't worry about spelling, punctuation, grammar and so on
- Give yourself permission to write anything
- Remember, whatever you write cannot be wrong – it's yours and no-one else needs to read it.

Bolton suggests other forms of writing in the subsequent four stages. Stage 2 involves thinking of an experience you have had and writing about it as if you are telling a story. In Stage 3, you can then read the story (and the six minutes of writing) and respond to it. In Stage 4, she suggests sharing what you have written with someone else – this needs to be someone you know well and trust (see Theme 5.2 on critical friendship). In Stage 5, she suggests you could begin to develop your work by writing from someone else's perspective – for example, from the client's point of view.

Try this   Now try doing one of Bolton's (2010) 'six minute writes'. Be sure to time yourself and to write freely. What are your reactions to this? For example, was it easier than you thought? More difficult than you thought? Too short a time or too long? And so on. Now check your writing against the two lists of points made in Theme 2.1. Does your writing fulfil the criteria for being described as reflective?

Theme 2.4 A structure for reflective writing

People who are new to reflective writing often find it helpful to have a structure for their writing. This can help them to make a start and will often then be discarded as writing reflectively becomes easier. Knott and Scragg (2011) offer a useful structure for writing a reflective journal, which can be helpful for people who are faced with the question, 'So what do I need to write?' Their structure is based on three stages, each with accompanying questions for clarity, which should encourage a deeper reflective approach.

Stage 1 – Reflection

Here the authors suggest that you focus on an issue or a concern that you have in relation to your practice. Like Bolton (2010), they advise that this is done freely and spontaneously in order to capture your thoughts.

Stage 2 – Analysis

This is the most complex of the stages and involves responding to the following key questions:

- What is happening here?
- What assumptions am I making?
- What does this show about my underlying beliefs about myself and my practice?
- What are some of the alternative ways of looking at this? (for example, from someone else's perspective). This particular aspect is similar to Bolton's (2010) Stage 5.

Stage 3 – Action

As this suggests, the focus here is on the action you take following the analysis. Again the authors suggest considering some key questions:

- What action can I take?
- How can I learn from what has happened?
- How would I respond if this situation occurred again?

- What does this experience tell me about my beliefs about myself and my practice?

Try this Now try using Knott and Scragg's (2011) structure for reflective writing. Focus on a concern you have at the moment in relation to your learning and development. Write something in response to each of the prompt questions. Once you have done this, again think about your response to this exercise (see the questions in the previous activity). Which of the two methods do you prefer? What are the reasons for your preferences?

Try this   Now look back to Theme 2.3 and try moving on to Stage 2 (Bolton, 2010) by writing a story of a recent experience you have had. If this does not come easily to you, imagine you are talking to a friend at the end of a busy day and what you would say. When you finish writing, think about what you feel you learned from this.

Learning from experience

This section will:

- Help you begin to understand how we learn from experience
- Introduce you to a number of theoretical models of experiential learning
- Encourage you to focus on positive experiences as well as problematic ones
- Help you to recognise that we do not always learn from experience

Driscoll's 'What?' model

When you are new to reflective practice, a simple, straightforward model can be a useful way of helping you to get started; Driscoll's (2007) 'What?' model is one of these. It has the following three steps:

- **What?** – Step 1 encourages you to write a description of an event that has happened in your professional practice.
- **So what?** – Step 2 involves carrying out an analysis of the event by reflecting on selected aspects of it.
- **Now what?** – Step 3 asks you to devise a number of proposed actions following the experience and in the light of what you have learned.

Driscoll's model, which reflects the work of Borton (1970), is drawn as a circle with arrows pointing clockwise, showing how the three stages follow on from one another. However, a number of arrows can be drawn following Stage 3 to illustrate a variety of actions that could be taken following an experience.

Driscoll has also formulated a number of useful trigger questions to help you to use the model effectively, including:

- **Step 1** – What was my reaction to the experience and what did others do who were involved?
- **Step 2** – Do I feel troubled? If so, in what way?
- **Step 3** – How can I modify my practice if I face a similar situation again and what are the main learning points that I can take from this?

Many people who are completely new to reflective practice find Driscoll's model a very useful starting point for their early reflections. It is simple and easy to remember. However, after a time you may find that you need to reflect at a deeper level in relation to your developing practice. So do not be afraid to use this model in the early days and then to move onto others. This will mean that your skills of reflection develop alongside the other key skills that you use in professional practice.

'Reflective practice brings huge rewards in helping you to see different perspectives and think about your experience in different ways.'

(Jasper, 2003: 197–8)

Theme 3.2 Kolb's Experiential Learning Cycle

Many writers on the subject of reflective practice use cycles to describe how we learn from experience. These cycles enable us to understand the process as well as developing the ability to improve our learning and professional practice over time.

Kolb's (1984) Experiential Learning Cycle gives insights into how we all learn from experience. There are four stages in the cycle which are depicted as following on from each other, as shown by the arrows in the diagram below.

Kolb argues that this cycle often (but not always) starts with a concrete experience that is reviewed through reflective observation. This is followed by abstract conceptualisation where new thoughts and ideas emerge, which are then tried out in active experimentation, ready for the next relevant experience. All of this may happen in a matter of moments, or over days,

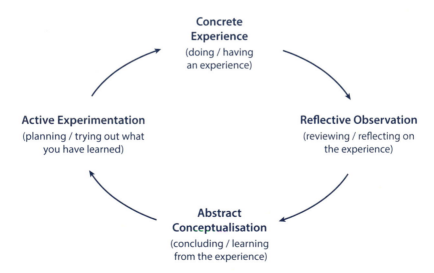

Figure 1 Kolb's Experiential Learning Cycle

weeks or months, depending on the experience. However, if you have particular learning preferences linked to your learning styles (see Theme 1) you may start the cycle at a different point. So, someone with a strong Reflector style will often spend time thinking before they act and start an experience. Theorists will often look for a model they can apply to an experience before embarking on it and Pragmatists usually like to plan before an experience whenever they can. Activists by contrast will often start at the top of the cycle.

Kolb argues that in order to learn the most from experience, we need to complete all four phases of the cycle, although it is important to understand that this will not necessarily always happen. For example, if we have a strong preference for a particular learning style, we can be tempted to skip points on the cycle. So, if something does not go well, a strong Activist may be tempted just to try again without spending time reflecting. A strong Reflector might spend too much time thinking about what happened, without learning from it and preparing for the next experience. A Theorist might be keen to try their favourite model again, convinced that it should work, and a Pragmatist could be tempted to be dismissive of something that they perceive does not work well in practice first time around.

It is also important to remember that any model that argues that things always happen in a particular order leaves itself open to critique – does it always happen like that? The answer is, probably not.

> 'Reflective practice facilitates learning by fostering a critical assessment of practice.'
>
> **(Ostermann and Kottkamp, 2004: 32)**

Theme 3.3   Do we always learn from experience?

In this journal we have begun to discuss professional learning in some detail. Of course, it is important to remember that we do not necessarily learn in every situation, and Jarvis's (1994) learning cycle is useful in this regard. Again based on the work of Kolb (1984) the cycle itself is significantly more complex than others, highlighting a range of different ways in which we can respond to an experience, including Memorisation and Practice Experimentation.

A particularly important element in Jarvis's evolution of Kolb's cycle is the notion that we do not always learn from experience; he calls this 'non-learning'. He argues that this can happen for the following three reasons:

- **Presumption** – This is a typical response to an everyday experience. We live much of our lives in a mechanical way, drawing on the bank of knowledge we have acquired through previous experience. In many situations we simply presume we know what to do based on what we have done before. It is worth remembering that life would simply be too tiring if we had to think about everything in detail.

- **Non-consideration** – This is a lack of response to a learning opportunity that presents itself to us, which can happen for a range of reasons. For example, we are too busy, we might fear the consequences of admitting we are unsure about something or we may simply lack understanding.

- **Rejection** – This is a conscious rejection of aspects of the experience that we could have learned from. The reasons for this happening can be similar to those identified above.

Jarvis highlights to us that learning from experience is not automatic and this acts as an important reminder that whether or not we engage in any kind of reflection always involves an element of choice. If we fail to engage in reflection, we can exit Jarvis's cycle prematurely, 'Reinforced but relatively unchanged', by simply tracking across the top of the cycle, rather than moving round it. Without some careful thought, over time, this could lead to a predisposition to non-learning.

Try this   Think of a situation that you have encountered recently where you failed to engage with learning from experience. Describe the situation and evaluate it, to find out why you did not learn from this experience. Does any of this resonate with Jarvis's (1994) reasons? Are there any other reasons you can add which are particular to your situation?

Problematic experiences or positive ones?

When it comes to discussing the kinds of experiences we learn the most from, authors differ in their approach. Here are two contrasting views as examples.

Osterman and Kottkamp's (2004) position is that we learn most from problematic experiences and argue that we need to focus on the kinds of situations that we encounter that cause us difficulties. As a result, the first step in their cycle (again based on the work of Kolb) requires us to identify a problem. This could be some form of discrepancy or gap between what happened and what we might have hoped for or expected. The second stage of 'observation and analysis' is the most important stage and the most complex, enabling us to gain a deeper understanding of the experience. This then leads on to the third stage of 'abstract reconceptualisation' where we search for new ideas and strategies, which are then experimented upon in the final stage of 'active experimentation'.

'Nobody is perfect and therefore reflection allows us to objectively seek alternative methods in order to reach our desired goals in our work.'

By contrast, Ghaye (2011:9) cautions against only focusing on problems using what he calls 'deficit-based' models of reflection and urges us to concentrate on positive experiences in order to avoid 'spirals of deficit-based actions'. Based on foundations of positive psychology, his strengths-based model offers an approach that encourages us to build on the positives by asking the following four questions:

1 What is successful right now? (**Appreciate**)
2 What do we need to change to make things better? (**Imagine**)
3 How can we achieve this? (**Design**)
4 Who needs to take action and what will the consequences be? (**Act**)

Whether we focus on problematic experiences or positive ones, reflecting on them will provide us with opportunities for growth and development. It is easy to see that focusing on one to the neglect of the other could mean that we become too negative or positive in our outlook. This could then be an argument for maintaining a balance between the two contrasting approaches.

Try this   Choose one of the learning cycles discussed in this section.
Now try applying it to an incident that has happened recently
as part of your work or training. How useful was the model? How
would you describe its strengths and weaknesses as a means of beginning to
evaluate your professional practice?

The practice of reflection

This section will:

- Help you begin to think about what it means to be a professional
- Introduce you to the key concepts of reflection on and in action
  - Introduce you to the concept of critical incident analysis
    - Help you begin to distinguish between espoused theories and theories in use

What does it mean to be a professional?

The word professional is one that we hear being used frequently, but what does it actually mean? Sometimes we hear people say, 'Well, that wasn't very professional, was it?' You may be on a course of professional training or be engaged in continuing professional development; either way it is worth spending some time considering what being a professional means.

Here are some thoughts. Being a professional means that:

- You have a body of knowledge in relation to your particular profession
- You work in a relatively autonomous way, without needing close supervision of every aspect of your work
- You are expected to show some initiative in your work
- You understand the boundaries of your role and have a clear grasp of when you need to refer to someone else
- You have the relevant skills to carry out your role well
- Your attitudes are in keeping with the profession that you belong to (for example, a caring or supportive or positive attitude, or indeed all of these)
- You adhere to the code of practice or ethics relevant for your profession
- Your work is not straightforward and will involve making professional judgments when you encounter situations where there are no clear right or wrong answers
- You aim to improve your practice all the time, reflecting on what you are doing and engaging in continuing professional development
- You aim to keep up to date with new knowledge and skills in relation to your practice.

'I cannot allow my relationships with clients to become personal and must be more professional in my dealings with them. I must not allow my judgement to be clouded; I have to work on this if I am going to be truly effective in my role.'

In his seminal work *The Reflective Practitioner*, Schön (1983) discusses Glazer's concept of major professions (medicine and law), near major professions (business and engineering) and minor professions (including social work and education). Major professions have traditionally relied on the application of science, based on the use of logic, or what Schön refers to as technical rationality. By contrast, Schön argues that those in the minor professions occupy the 'swampy lowlands' where practice is messy and often confusing, as there will not always be a logical solution. Whatever kind of profession you are involved in, even a relatively scientific one, when working with people your work will not always be predictable. Coping with this is a central aspect of what being a professional involves.

Theme 4.2 Reflection on action and reflection in action

Schön's (1983) work is seminal in relation to reflective practice and in his text, *The Reflective Practitioner*, he describes two important types of reflection; reflection on action and reflection in action. Both are important for people working in the minor professions, where typically there is no single correct response to a situation and no 'one size fits all' model that can be learned and applied in all situations and circumstances.

Reflection on action involves looking back on an experience and helps you to:

- analyse what happened
- think through the event from a number of perspectives (for example, your own and the client's)
- identify the things that went well
- identify problems and work towards solutions where possible
- identify areas for development
- build your professional knowledge
- think about what you would do next time in a similar situation.

Another important aspect of reflection on action is that it can prevent your practice from routine stagnation, by encouraging you to turn off your 'automatic pilot'. This is not meant to imply that you will need, or indeed be able to spend time reflecting on everything that happens. However, it is well worth thinking about when and how you will make time to include this in your professional life, in order to keep your practice (and your working life generally) vibrant.

The second type of reflection that Schön (1983) discusses is reflection in action. All of us spend time thinking – it is so much part of our everyday lives that sometimes we do not even realise we are doing it. Reflection in action is the kind of thinking we all do as we are working, studying and living generally; as human beings we have a capacity to think whilst doing other things. When writing about reflection in action, Schön describes it as 'thinking on your feet'.

When working with people it will often be necessary to try a number of different strategies to enable them to engage with you as you work with them. By reflecting in action, you will be able to assess the strategies you are using as you go along, deciding whether or not your approach is working with that particular individual or group. If not, you will need to change your approach to try and find something that will work.

Schön, of course, is not without his critics. Whether or not it is possible to distinguish clearly between reflection on and in action is debatable. Indeed, in his own writing Schön himself is not absolutely clear on this distinction. However, as concepts they are often useful in helping us to analyse practice at a deeper level.

'Reflection in action is where we may reflect in the midst of action without interrupting it. Our thinking serves to reshape what we are doing while we are doing it.'

(Schön, 1987: 26)

Critical incident analysis

When reflecting on action, it is often helpful to focus on a particular experience or event and to examine it carefully. This is often referred to as critical incident analysis. A critical incident is something which we interpret as a problem or a challenge in a particular context, rather than just a routine occurrence (see Osterman and Kottkamp, 2004; and Theme 3.4). Usually it will be something that gives you some kind of inner discomfort – it may often make you stop and question what you should do next. You may find yourself thinking something like 'OK, so what on earth do I do now?', as some kind of gap in your knowledge is exposed.

Critical incident analysis is an approach to dealing with the challenges that everyday practice brings. If we are aiming to practice reflectively, we need to be prepared to pose questions about our practice in order to problematise it. So, for example, rather than simply describing what happened, you should be prepared to question why it happened as it did, and think about it from a number of different perspectives as well as your own. This will also involve refusing to accept 'what is' and being open to seeing things differently and to making changes. We need to explore incidents that occur in our day-to-day work in order to understand them better and find alternative ways of reacting and responding to them. Such incidents can have a significant impact on our personal and professional learning.

> '*In life we all have encounters and experiences which make us pause and possibly re-evaluate how we see and deal with certain events. Professionals call these times critical incidents.*'

A critical incident is usually personal to an individual. Incidents only become critical (that is, problematic) if the individual sees them in this way; what is problematic for one person may not be for someone else. The incident is defined as critical after the event and it is worth remembering that we may often feel negative about any such incident. It is important to get beyond any uncomfortable feelings this may cause, so that learning and development can occur.

'Reflection is an important human activity in which people recapture their experience, think about it, mull it over and evaluate it.'

(Boud et al., 1985: 19)

Espoused theories and theories in use

Schön spent a significant amount of time working with Argyris and together they took some important steps forward in gaining a deeper understanding of experiential learning. In their work (Argyris and Schön, 1974) they argue that two types of theory are at work in professional practice. They are as follows:

- **Espoused theories** – these are conscious and public. If we are in a situation where we are asked to explain our actions or our plans, we will use our espoused theories to explain what we did and why. Espoused theories are explicit and describe what we say we do.
- **Theories in use** – Argyris and Schön argue that people operate with mental maps that help them to know how to think and act in certain situations. These maps are established over time and are based on our previous experiences and our assumptions regarding such things as what works and what does not. When taking action, we draw on our theories in use. Theories in use are implicit and describe what we actually do as distinct from what we say we do.

In practice there is often a discrepancy or gap between our espoused theories and our theories in use. It could be argued that the role of reflection is to reveal the theories in use and to explore the nature of the gap. This will enable us to work towards congruence (or genuineness) in our thoughts and actions. Whilst the two remain connected in some way, the gap creates a catalyst for reflection that can lead to change. However, if the gap between the two is too wide this can become a problem.

Our theories in use are closely linked with what Schön (1983: 50) refers to as knowing-in-action, which is tacit knowledge. If you ask a very experienced practitioner why they did something in a particular way, many will need some time to think about their reasons before being able to articulate them. Their first response could be something like 'well, I'm not sure; I just did it that way.' In short, their practice has become automatic and somewhat intuitive because of their range and depth of professional experience. Whilst this is immensely useful, it is also worth remembering that this is where bad habits could begin to creep in.

Try this Imagine you are facing a difficult issue in relation to your professional practice – use a real-life example if you can. Now write down how you will respond to this under the two headings of your espoused theories and your theories in use. Now highlight the similarities and differences between what you have written under each heading.

Try this Describe a time recently when you were very conscious that you had to reflect in action or 'think on your feet'. How easy or difficult was this at the time? Describe it as a series of steps and then focus on the changes in your thinking and in the strategies you were using at the time. How did this help you to build your tacit knowing-in-action?

Learning from feedback

This section will:

- Help you to understand what constitutes good and bad feedback

- Introduce you to the concept of critical friendship

- Introduce you to the Johari Window model for feedback and self-disclosure

- Help you to think about the settings where feedback can occur

Theme 5.1 What makes good feedback?

Good feedback is vital for professional growth and development, so it is important to understand what it is and what it is not. On professional courses and in professional practice generally you will receive feedback and also be asked to give it.

Good feedback is:

- Respectful
- Helpful and supportive
- Honest
- Specific and focused on behaviour that can be changed or developed
- Timely
- Limited in amount – there is only so much feedback that a person can cope with at any one time
- Clear and clarified if necessary, to avoid misunderstandings
- Focused on positives with some points for further development to enable the person to make progress
- Motivating.

Good feedback is not:

- Hurtful
- Accusatory
- Unhelpful
- Undermining
- Judgmental
- General and focused on personal issues
- Too much to take in at once
- Vague and woolly
- Only focused on negatives.

Understanding what makes good and bad feedback is important for two reasons. First, it helps you to process feedback when you receive it. Suffice it to say that not all feedback is good for the reasons identified above. When receiving feedback it is important to examine it in order to discern its validity. Second, it enables you to give good feedback to others.

When thinking about a model for engaging in feedback, the idea of the 'praise sandwich' can be helpful. In other words, begin with some positives, then focus on some areas for development or things that could be done better, and finish with a summary of the positives. Remember that it is very difficult for someone to move forward in their development if they only receive negative messages. Such messages often start with words like 'but'. Changing this by using words like 'and instead you could' can make a real difference to how someone receives feedback and subsequently uses it. Everyone needs positive points to build on.

Feedback given in the form of the 'praise sandwich' boosts confidence, builds self-esteem and helps someone to see where they can improve. Confidence is a very delicate thing – difficult to gain but very easy to destroy. It is always worth remembering this whenever you are asked to give or receive feedback.

The 'praise sandwich' is, of course, not without its critics. For example, once it becomes obvious, people can either focus on the criticism and forget the praise, or do the opposite and focus only on the praise and fail to hear any criticisms. If too much praise is given and little criticism, people can get the impression that everything was OK, when this may not have been the case. This is an easy trap to fall into if you need to give some challenging feedback to someone at any point. If too little praise is given, it can be seen as tokenistic and appear insincere, in which case it is likely to be ignored. Feedback that involves praise followed by development points using words like 'as well as' and 'you could develop this by…' will be constructive, supportive and developmental.

Theme 5.2 Critical friendship

There are things in life that a good friend should and will tell you; as such, a friend is honest whilst being caring in their approach. While you are studying on your course or as part of your continuing professional development, you may be asked to work with a critical friend; this is a person who can help you engage with many aspects of your growing self-awareness. Working with a critical friend will help you gain valuable feedback on your practice, mirroring the kind of relationship you may have with a supervisor. It is therefore important to choose a critical friend carefully.

So, what makes a good critical friend? They should be:

- Someone who you know and can trust
- Someone who puts you at ease
- A good listener
- Someone who asks good questions that challenge your thinking
- Someone who acts with integrity
- Someone who is positive, constructive and encouraging
- Someone who is willing to point out negatives as well as positives.

The core qualities of critical friendship are:

- Respect for each other
- Trust
- Openness
- Honesty
- A good rapport.

'I was very relieved when we were asked to choose a "critical friend" to help throughout this journey. Now I felt like I had someone to go to and, equally, they could come to me.'

A vital key to becoming an effective critical friend is to remember to take a sensitive and questioning approach. A critical friend is not there to be negative or destructive, but rather to help their friend to examine critically their approach in any given situation. Often a good place to start is to ask the important 'why' question. This should not be asked in an accusatory way, such as 'why on earth did you do that?', but in a constructive, enquiring way, for example, 'what made you respond in that way?'

It is important to spend some time thinking about who your critical friend could be – it is worth remembering that it may not be your best friend. It should be someone who you can rely on to give you open and honest feedback, even if there may be aspects that you do not want to hear. In the long run, this will be of greater benefit to your professional development than working with someone who finds it difficult to question the more challenging aspects of your practice.

'Unless one is prepared to receive, indeed actively seek, feedback – which may be adverse or distressing – one will continue to misread situations and deceive oneself that one's own actions are the best in the circumstances …. However, it is not only obtaining good feedback that matters, but making good use of it by being open to new interpretations which challenge one's assumptions.'

(Eraut, 1994: 116)

The Johari Window

Feedback will be important in your professional development, as it will ensure that you are not operating in a vacuum. The Johari Window was developed by Joseph Luft and Harry Ingham and is a model which helps us to gain useful insights into how we relate to other people; this can give us greater self-awareness regarding how we communicate with others in groups. The Johari Window (Luft, 1984) is depicted below.

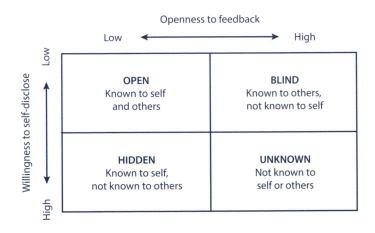

Figure 2 The Johari Window

The model depicts how feedback and self-disclosure can help us to gain greater self-awareness. Being open to feedback and engaging in receiving it will enable you to become aware of those things that others know about you, but you do not necessarily know about yourself. Similarly, being willing to self-disclose will enable others to get to know you better. In both instances, such actions mean that the Open area becomes larger as the vertical line moves to the right and the horizontal line moves down.

All professionals need to be open to feedback for their professional growth and development. The right amount of self-disclosure at the right time can build empathy in a helping relationship. But remember, in any professional situation self-disclosure is always a choice and you should never disclose something unless you are comfortable doing so. Indeed, in some professional settings self-disclosure is seen as problematic, as it could be a distraction from the needs of the person you are working with. So you should always self-disclose with caution.

Giving feedback and receiving it along with self-disclosure always involves an element of risk, so it is important that it is done in an atmosphere of trust. Some people argue that the overall goal is to expand the Open area as much as possible. However, it is important to remember that it is certainly possible to be too open and to disclose too much. In professional practice it is appropriate that some things remain in the Hidden area; for example, how you might feel about a particular client's behaviour or outlook. Some things are disclosed more appropriately only in supervision or with a more experienced colleague.

'Guided reflection is
defined as reflection that,
through the questioning and insights
of another more experienced practitioner,
can get beneath the surface of experience.'
(Howatson-Jones, 2010: 110)

The settings where feedback can occur

We have already established that feedback will be an important facet of your professional development. Eraut (2006) usefully describes the following four different settings where feedback can occur:

- **Immediate and *in situ*** – this is feedback that is given during or immediately following an experience and is given by a colleague or someone who witnessed the event. It is usually specific and can focus on the factors that influenced the particular situation, which can often be forgotten later.

- **Informal conversations away from the workplace or place of study** – feedback here can be intentional or unintentional and can depend on the learning culture with the given situation.

- **Mentoring and supervision** – here feedback is more formal and related to performance. The mentor or supervisor will not always have direct opportunities to observe the work they are asked to supervise.

- **Appraisal** – more formal and less frequent feedback, which relates to the achievement of goals and objectives set previously.

Eraut is clear that receiving feedback will not always be a positive experience and, in fact, at times it can even be distressing. However, it is vital for professional development; without it we can deceive ourselves into thinking such things as, 'I did the best I could in the circumstances', or, 'I must have misunderstood what was required. If things had been clearer, I would have known what to do.' He also points to the need to use feedback, rather than simply receive it. This highlights the issue of choice; listening, taking stock and acting on feedback when we feel it is justified and appropriate will always involve making a decision. Engaging in the feedback process means that we will be able to learn from the experiences of others. This could alter our perceptions and help us to begin to see things differently.

'Reflective practice itself, or even the study of it, can lead you to think of things that you know you should try but maybe are afraid to.'

Try this Now think of a time when you received what you felt was useful feedback on an aspect of your professional development. What was good about it and how did it help you? How far did the feedback fulfil the criteria for good feedback in Theme 5.1? Now go through a similar process focusing on some poor feedback you have received.

Try this Have a discussion with your critical friend about your progress. Afterwards, think about your discussion in relation to the Johari Window. How did you seek feedback and what was your response to it? How much were you prepared to engage in self-disclosure? What were the reasons for this?

Feelings and professional practice

This section will:

- Introduce you to the Almond Effect
- Help you to understand that our memories and feelings are stored together in our brains
- Introduce you to two models of reflection that focus on feelings as a source of learning

Theme **6.1** The Almond Effect

As human beings we all have emotional responses to people and situations. However, we often fail to understand what triggers these responses and why they can be so powerful at any given time. No doubt we have all experienced situations where we have said things or reacted in a certain way and have immediately regretted what we have said or done. Riches (2012) explains that the reason this happens is because of what she calls the Almond Effect.

Neuroscience shows that the human brain is designed to respond to threatening situations with a 'flight or fight' response. These responses are usually automatic and are the result of the hard-wiring of our neural pathways. They have been learned through the process of evolution and have played a vital part in the survival of the human race. Coming from the Greek word for almond, the amygdalae (we each have two of them) are almond-shaped parts of the brain that play a vital role in stimulating and regulating our emotional responses to situations and people, particularly in relation to fear. In short, they prompt a 'fight or flight' response where appropriate. Because of our amygdalae we can also sense emotional responses in other people. Our instinctive emotional responses always happen first, followed by our rational responses.

Riches describes a 'Mindfield', where the Almond Effect prompts us to respond emotionally, before we have had the opportunity to think things through; often this results in saying or doing things that we might regret. In her book, Riches discusses a range of strategies to help us to slow down and to reach a more rational position. These include the following:

- Noticing any physical signs, such as an increase in your heart rate, trembling or blushing
- Breathing deeply before responding
- Being aware of your body language and keeping it open.

It is always worth remembering that, as human beings, we are emotional first and rational second.

Try this   Think of an incident that has happened recently which has prompted a strong emotional reaction in you. Describe the incident and try to identify what might have prompted such a strong response. What does this tell you about situations like this and how you will cope in the future?

Theme 6.2   Memories and feelings

In his early work on Transactional Analysis, Eric Berne was influenced by the work of Wilder Penfield, a neuro-surgeon from McGill University in Montreal, Canada. During his career, Penfield carried out a large number of experiments whilst operating on conscious patients suffering from focal epilepsy. He did this in order to learn more about how the human brain functions, particularly in relation to how memories are stored.

Penfield found that by touching particular parts of the temporal cortex with a galvanic probe, patients were prompted to speak about memories that came into focus. They described what they recollected vividly and in detail. In addition, they also described how they felt. As a result, Penfield concluded that memories and feelings are stored together in the brain. In other words, when we remember things, we not only remember how we felt, but also experience those feelings (or at least some of them) again.

At times, we might remember something and this memory prompts us to feel what we felt at that time. At other times, we might have a particular feeling and it can take us some time to link it to a previous experience or time in our lives. These feelings can often be triggered by an event or by one of our senses – for example, a piece of music that we hear or a particular smell. However, this happens, Penfield's research shows that memories and feelings are stored together in the brain and that one cannot be evoked without the other.

In relation to professional practice, having an understanding of this is helpful for two reasons. First, we should expect our feelings to come to the surface and not always be able to understand immediately why this is happening. Time spent in reflection, either alone or with others, will often help us to remember our past experiences and the feelings associated with them. This means that we can begin to process them. Second, we should not be surprised by instances where our work with clients causes us to have feelings that we do not expect. These feelings can be linked with reminders from our past that we can then begin to rationalise.

'The expression of
feelings is always cathartic.
The issue is not so much removing
them but accepting them as valid and
harnessing this energy for taking
positive action.'

(Johns, 2010: 37)

Theme 6.3 Gibbs' Reflective Cycle

Having considered the role of our feelings in professional practice, we can use theoretical models to help us to understand more about how we process these. Gibbs' (1998) Reflective Cycle is particularly useful and is depicted below.

Figure 3 Gibbs' Reflective Cycle

Many people find the prompt questions on the cycle particularly helpful in making the model practical and easy to apply to their work. For those who are supporting people in challenging circumstances, the second point on the cycle with its focus on feelings is particularly important. It would be foolish to think that a professional practitioner who is asked to work in an empathic way would not have emotional responses to the situations of their clients. As we know, this is not how we function as human beings.

It is worth noting that the third step on the cycle, 'Evaluation', encourages us to examine what was positive about the experience as well as what was negative. Some people have a tendency to be too hard on themselves, focusing only on the negative aspects of experiences. As Ghaye (2011) argues (see Theme 3.4), we also need to recognise things that have gone well and to build on these.

The fourth step on the cycle is also worth noting, as it is different from other cycles we have examined so far. Here, Gibbs urges us to engage in analysis in order to make sense of what happened. The tentative wording he chooses, 'What sense can you make out of the situation' (as distinct from 'What sense do you make out of the situation?') seems to imply that the experiences we have in professional practice and the situations we face will not always make sense. However, he encourages us to try to make sense of them in order to deepen our understandings.

'By reflecting on my own feelings about a situation, I am beginning to feel less stressed about things that are beyond my control.'

When comparing Gibbs' cycle with that of Kolb, it is clear that there are similarities and differences between them. Like Kolb's cycle, Gibbs also suggests that learning from experience happens in a particular sequence of steps. However, Gibbs' model is more detailed in that it has six points on it compared to Kolb's four. Gibbs' emphasis on feelings takes reflection to a deeper level and can be seen as a key milestone on the road from reflective practice to critically reflective practice.

Processing feelings

In their book *Reflection: Turning Experience into Learning*, Boud, Keogh and Walker (1985) put forward a very useful reflective cycle that focuses on feelings. As human beings, we all have emotional responses to situations and Boud et al. encourage us to pay attention to our feelings in order to process them.

'Writing has helped me to make sense of things, especially why I am feeling a particular way. It is something I will definitely carry on, I'm not as stressed as I was which is a positive.'

Their reflective cycle has the following three stages.

- **Returning to the experience** – this involves recollecting what happened and could include discussing it with others.
- **Attending to feelings** – there are two important aspects in relation to paying attention to feelings here: building on positive feelings and removing negative or obstructive ones.
- **Re-evaluating the experience** – this is the most important stage, where new knowledge is added to existing knowledge and incorporated within it.

In contrast to Gibbs, Boud et al. use the term 'stages' rather than 'steps' and their model is designed to be multi-directional – highlighting how professionals often move forwards and backwards within the process of reflection as their analysis of their practice becomes deeper.

It is important to note that unless we attend to our feelings and take action to process them, it is likely that negative or obstructive ones, in particular, will remain and could then act as a barrier to our professional practice and development. Processing feelings involves externalising them and how we do this is a matter of choice, like many other areas of professional development. It is important to work out what helps you as an individual. Writing in a journal like this can be therapeutic and can help you to engage in the process of externalising your feelings. For some people, writing about their feelings on paper helps them to leave them there, literally and metaphorically. For others, discussion and supervision (see Theme 9) has the same effect. The vital thing to emphasise is that it is the processing of feelings that is important, not how it is done.

'Of particular importance
within description is the
observation of the feeling evoked during
the experience. On occasions our emotional
reactions can override our rationality to such an
extent that we react unwarily and with blurred
perceptions.'

(Boud, Keogh and Walker, 1985: 28)

Try this   Now try using one of the reflective cycles (Gibbs, 1998 or Boud, Keogh and Walker, 1985) to evaluate your learning from this incident. Which one did you choose and why? How useful was it in helping you to deal with the emotional issues raised by the incident?

Assumptions

This section will:

- Introduce you to the keys terms reflection, reflectivity and reflexivity
- Introduce you to the concept of double-loop learning
- Discuss how we can challenge our assumptions by using the Ladder of Inference
- Discuss Mezirow's seven levels of reflectivity that can lead to perspective transformation

Theme 7.1 Double-loop learning

In Theme 3, we examined Kolb's (1984) Experiential Learning Cycle. In this process, we have an experience, reflect on it, draw out some general principles and any new knowledge that can then be applied as we prepare for the next experience. This type of learning is valuable in day to day professional practice and can be described as 'single-loop learning' (Argyris and Schön, 1974).

However, in order to take professional learning to a deeper level we need to begin to challenge our own assumptions and our established ways of doing things. Assumptions are things that over time we have begun to take for granted. We do this to such an extent that we no longer question them or even think about them. In many circumstances, assumptions are valuable as they prevent us from needing to think about every aspect of our lives in

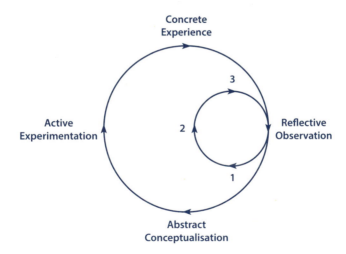

1. Am I jumping to conclusions? What assumptions am I making?
2. Are my assumptions justifiable?
3. How should my perceptions change?

Figure 4 Double-loop learning

detail. For example, if we had to think closely regarding what to do each time we made a cup of tea, life would be exhausting! Instead, we draw on our past experiences and make it somewhat automatically. However, if we apply this to professional practice with people, this kind of 'automatic pilot' becomes very risky, as it is here that prejudice and discriminatory practices can be rooted.

Critically reflective practice encourages us to delve beneath the surface of our long-held ideas and paradigms, in order to challenge our assumptions. Here, the concept of double-loop learning (Argyris and Schön, 1974) is very helpful.

Unlike Kolb's single loop, double-loop learning asks us to bring our assumptions to the surface, to challenge them and to question the things that we take for granted (see Figure 4 on the previous page). This can lead us to question our personal values and beliefs that lie beneath professional practice (see Theme 8). As a result, through this process, our habitual ways of thinking about things can change and practice can become more creative.

Questioning our assumptions as part of reflective observation is always personally and professionally challenging. It can be done by asking questions such as:

- What assumptions am I making in this situation?
- Am I jumping to conclusions?
- Are my assumptions justifiable?
- Do my perceptions need to change?

Like Schön's reflection on and in action, this type of questioning can be done during an experience (in action) or afterwards (on action).

'Assumptions are taken-
for-granted beliefs about the world
and our place within it, that seem so obvious
to us as not to need stating explicitly.'

(Brookfield, 1995: 2)

Theme 7.2   Reflection, reflectivity and reflexivity

In the early part of this journal, we used the term 'reflection' to denote the kind of thinking professionals undertake in order to evaluate their practice. As we now move towards having an understanding of critically reflective practice, two more words require some clarification: 'reflectivity' and 'reflexivity'. This is not straightforward as these terms are similar and can sometimes, rather confusingly, be used interchangeably in literature.

- **Reflection** – this is the term used by many writers on the subject of reflective practice, including Schön, his colleagues and his associates. It refers to the thinking processes that we engage in as learners and professionals and can be deliberate or otherwise.
- **Reflectivity** – this is the deliberate act of engaging in the process of thinking in order to analyse and evaluate an aspect of professional practice. This is sometimes referred to as the doing of reflection.
- **Reflexivity** – refers to the high level of self-awareness needed to practice in an anti-discriminatory way. It involves becoming aware of our values and assumptions, which are culturally situated. Fook (2004) argues that such awareness demands that we look inwards and outwards, recognising that every part of ourselves, including our context, affects how we practice.

Reflexivity is vital for all professionals who want to become critically reflective practitioners. In all situations this will involve being aware of issues of power in relationships and in institutions and seeking to shift the balance of power where appropriate.

Try this Think of a recent example from your practice where you engaged in double-loop learning to question your assumptions. What did you conclude about your assumptions? Were they accurate and appropriate in this instance?

Theme 7.3   Argyris' Ladder of Inference

Each of us at some point in time has been guilty of making assumptions and jumping to conclusions. To begin to challenge our assumptions, it is important to understand how assumptions are made. The Ladder of Inference (Argyris, 1982) is a very helpful way of looking at this. In his excellent video clip on the Group Harmonics website, Ed Luzio (2011) draws the diagram below:

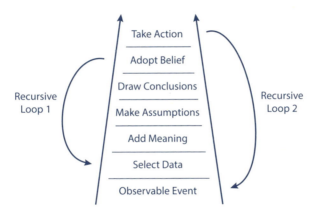

Figure 5 *Argyris' Ladder of Inference*

At the foot of the ladder, we observe an event as it happens. The human brain receives so many messages each day that we select the data we need or want at any given time. We then add meaning to that data from our current situation and our past experiences in similar circumstances. The meaning we add is drawn from the perspective of our own personal and cultural settings. This leads us to make assumptions and, from there, to draw conclusions about the person or the situation. These conclusions then become part of our beliefs about the world and how it operates. The action we then take is based on our beliefs.

Following on from this, we can take one of two recursive loops. The first is from our beliefs to the second step of the ladder. Here, our beliefs lead us to make choices about the data we select in the future. In short, we usually select the data that confirms our existing beliefs and ignore the data that does not. The second loop is from action to the bottom of the ladder. Here, we take action to seek more observable data. But the data we gather is also based on our beliefs, which encourage us to see what we have seen before. This makes our approach biased in favour of what we have seen previously. By following either of these recursive loops, our assumptions are confirmed and our existing beliefs are reinforced.

Here is an example. Someone you are working with (a client, patient, student) behaves badly and you select data from what you observe. You only see their bad behaviour rather than anything good they might do. The meaning you add is that you are not surprised that they behave badly as many people you work with in this particular context behave like this. You then make assumptions about the person based on this; for example, that people in this context always behave badly and this particular person is no different. From this, you draw your own conclusions that whenever you work in this particular context, you need to expect to deal with difficult people. These conclusions form the basis of your beliefs, which in turn influence your future actions. In your actions, you are then most likely to select the data that confirms your existing beliefs. Without even realising, you get to the point where you see what you expect to see, rather than what actually happens.

This habit can be avoided by consciously going to the bottom of the ladder, and either to regularly question the assumptions you make and the conclusions that you draw from them or, alternatively, seek out some contrary data that will disconfirm your assumptions. In the example above, you could seek out some evidence for positive behaviour to disprove your beliefs. This is a vital step in working towards anti-discriminatory practice and it is an important element of critically reflective practice.

Mezirow's seven levels of reflectivity

The feelings we have about the people we encounter often stem from our attitudes and values, which can then affect how well we engage with them and the expectations we have of them. In Theme 6, we examined Boud, Keogh and Walker's (1985) model of reflection. In their work, they take us beyond the acknowledgement of feelings into the realm of examining our attitudes and values and the ways in which these, along with the assumptions we make, can be reinforced through experience.

'My assumptions blurred my vision.'

Citing the work of Mezirow (1978; 1981) they describe the following seven levels of reflectivity, which help us to examine how we approach people and situations: in particular, the assumptions we might make as a result of past experiences. The first four levels operate within our ordinary consciousness and include an examination of our feelings and values. The remaining three levels lie within the realm of critical consciousness and include becoming aware of the reasons why we might be quick to make judgments about situations and people. The seven levels are as follows:

1 **Reflectivity** – becoming aware of how we see things, and how we think and act. What do I think and feel about this person and how does this affect my behaviour?

2 **Affective Reflectivity** – becoming aware of our feelings about how we think and act. How do I feel about the way I think/act in relation to them?

3 **Discriminant Reflectivity** – questioning whether or not our perceptions about people are accurate. Are my perceptions of them correct?

4 **Judgemental Reflectivity** – becoming aware of our value judgements. What assumptions am I making about people and their situation based on my values?

5 **Conceptual Reflectivity** – questioning the constructs we use when we think about other people. For example, just because the person does X, will Y always follow?

6 **Psychic Reflectivity** – recognising our own prejudices that can make us quick to make judgements about people on the basis of limited information about them. Am I jumping to conclusions?

7 **Theoretical Reflectivity** – becoming aware that the reasons we are quick to make judgements about people are based on cultural and psychological assumptions. What are my assumptions about this person based on?

By examining our thinking at each level, we can begin to question our assumptions, in particular whether they are accurate or not. This means we can challenge our assumptions where we feel they are not justifiable and reframe them where appropriate. Mezirow asserts that assumptions are always culturally situated and that by reaching the deepest level of Theoretical Reflectivity, some perspective transformation can happen. In other words, reflecting at this level means that I begin to think about things differently.

'Reflective practice is
a process that involves a
reflective turn. This means returning
to look again at our taken-for-granted
values, professional understandings and
practices.'

(Ghaye and Ghaye, 1998: 16)

Try this   Think of a time recently where it became clear that you had made some inaccurate assumptions. What happened? When and how did you become aware of the assumptions you were making? Now use either Argyris' Ladder of Inference or Mezirow's seven levels of reflectivity to analyse your thought processes and your actions in relation to this. How might the outcome have been different if you had not made these assumptions? What can you learn from this?

Ethics and values

This section will:

- Introduce you to the keys terms, 'ethics' and 'values'
- Introduce you to the concept of Transactional Analysis drivers
- Help you to think about the impact of your values on your professional practice
- Establish the importance of considering issues of power in professional practice

Theme 8.1   Ethics and values – what's the difference?

In order to practise in a critically reflective way, an understanding of your own values is important. Often the assumptions we make about people and situations (see Theme 7) are based on our values, so having an understanding of them will be vital in professional practice. Many professional courses include modules on ethics and values and, as part of these, a range of theoretical approaches are considered. The terms themselves are complex and not easy to define, but Knowles and Lander's (2012) work provides a helpful and practical introduction to this whole area.

In discussing definitions of ethics and values, Knowles and Lander (2012) suggest that values are things that we feel are important to us – in a literal sense, they are things that we value. These values are linked with our beliefs about the world and how it should operate. Ethics, then, are sets of rules that help us to know how to act and behave correctly in relation to our values. Here is a very simple example: I value honesty and believe it to be important, so I do not tell lies.

Values can be personal and professional. Our personal values are deep-rooted and will often stem from those things that we have learned to recognise as being important, usually from a very young age. Such values can include things like honesty, hard work and the importance of family. Personal values are always culturally situated and reflect the social context of the individual. Professional values are approaches to practice that are accepted by a particular profession as being central to the way work is carried out. Often, these are enshrined in codes of practice that a practitioner agrees to abide by in their work and provide the foundations of professional practice. Such codes often also contain codes of ethics, which detail how things need to be done in order for these values to be demonstrated.

However, any consideration of ethics and values will always be challenging. Here are two areas for thought. The simple example given above might appear to be straightforward, but does this mean that I never lie? Are there situations where not being honest could be justifiable? In relation to professional practice, you may well be able to think of examples where your own personal values could be at odds with your professional values. These are often referred to as ethical dilemmas, where there will not be a simple straightforward answer as to how you should proceed. Here taking a critically reflective approach is vital.

'Action that is informed and linked to certain values ... emphasises the requirement to make a positive difference to clients, to avoid "automatic pilot" and to strive to develop responsive, purposeful and understanding practice.'

(Bulman, 2008: 7)

Transactional Analysis drivers

The concept of drivers is important in Transactional Analysis (TA) and recognising them and the influences they have on our work and lives can be extremely helpful. Put simply, drivers can be seen as consistent messages we received from our parents or carers when we were growing up. They consist of commands about what to do and what not to do, how we should behave and how we should not, plus definitions of people and the world. Taibi Kahler put these messages together into five groups called drivers. Drivers become powerful psychological tools and have a big influence on how we live our lives – in other words, they drive us.

The five TA drivers are shown below. Each driver has strengths and weaknesses associated with it; weaknesses often emanate from strengths that are overdone. Here are some examples:

- **Be Perfect** – accurate, eye for detail, neat and tidy but will be harsh on themselves and 'beat themselves up' when they don't meet their own exacting standards, and can be harsh on others too.
- **Be Strong** – excellent in a crisis, dependable, makes people feel safe and secure, but doesn't tend to show their feelings so may come across as aloof and disinterested.
- **Try Hard** – has a strong work ethic, is persistent and resilient but sometimes does not know when to stop if something is too difficult and is not comfortable when receiving praise.
- **Please (people)** – great team member who gets on well with lots of people, but does not want to upset people so can be unassertive and have a desire to rescue people.
- **Hurry Up** – enthusiastic, achieves a lot in a short space of time, but can be prone to make mistakes through rushing and lack of forethought.

Recognising our own TA drivers makes us more self-aware. At the same time an understanding of them can help us become more aware of how others are behaving and communicating. As in other areas of professional development, it is important to focus on the strengths of the drivers, whilst seeking to minimise their weaknesses.

Try this   Consider the descriptions of each of the five drivers. Which would you say is most and least like you? What new insights does this give you about yourself and your relationships with others?

The impact of values on professional work

We have established that everyone has personal values and that these have an impact on professional practice. One question that then arises is whether or not an individual can be completely neutral (or in other words remain completely objective) in their professional work with people. In the context of counselling, Corey, Schneider Corey and Callanan (2007) discuss the concept of therapeutic neutrality, which can usefully be taken into other professional arenas. They discuss a two-way process; the ways in which our values affect our work with clients, and vice versa, and what can happen when the two sets of values are in conflict with one another.

They also pose some questions that are helpful to think about. Firstly, is it possible to keep our values out of the professional helping process? Many people today would argue that it is not possible because our values are an integral part of our make-up. Secondly, if it were possible, would it be helpful to set our values aside? Corey et al. argue that this is not desirable as the sharing of values can in itself be helpful, encouraging people to think through their own positions on a range of issues.

> 'Reflection has certainly made me more aware of my own attitudes and the impact of my own behaviour on the feelings of others.'

The most important point they make is that if we take the stance that neutrality is not possible, professional practitioners need to have a clear understanding of their own values and the impact these have on their work. These values can then be discussed openly. This helps the client to know where the professional practitioner is coming from and means that the person can explore their own values. However, sharing values should not be done as a way of influencing the person concerned. A discussion of values will include such things as clarifying assumptions and articulating core beliefs and this will often be challenging for all concerned.

Try this Now think about instances recently where you feel your values have been challenged, for example through working with clients in particularly difficult situations. Describe your responses to these challenges. How has this helped you gain greater self-awareness?

Theme 8.4 Anti-discriminatory practice

Critically reflective practice involves an acknowledgement of issues of power that are present in all relationships. In order to examine how such issues are played out in society, Thompson (2012) outlines his PCS model, which helps us to understand how inequalities and discrimination are perpetuated in society. This model contains the following three levels.

- **Personal** – these are our individual thoughts and feelings and the behaviours that emanate from them. Our personal attitudes and values, or our ways of perceiving things and people, are also part of this level and include prejudices that we might hold about certain people and situations. To some extent this level is shaped by our previous personal experiences.
- **Cultural** – culture relates to things that are shared by people. This includes shared understandings and meanings as well as the way things are done in certain contexts. All of this leads to patterns of behaviour that are deemed to be acceptable or unacceptable within that particular social setting. At this level a wide range of assumptions are made and much is taken for granted without any questioning.
- **Structural** – this operates at the social level; in other words it relates to the ways in which society is organised and divided and is linked closely with issues of power. People with power usually like to keep it and to stop others from gaining it; in short, this is oppression. This process means that oppression and discrimination become institutionalised, or in Thompson's words, '"sewn in" to the fabric of society' (2012: 34).

Thompson argues that discrimination happens at every level of PCS with each level being interlinked and reinforcing the other. Critically reflective practice involves recognising our own values at the Personal level, the ways things are done at the Cultural level and any inequalities that operate at a Structural level, particularly within our own institutions. As with all aspects of reflective practice, we are then faced with choices to make, regarding possible action.

'What I am proposing
is reflection that enhances
human insight, and practices that enable
us to positively draw upon such insight to better
understand our work, to amplify success, and to
focus on doing more of what is valued.'

(Ghaye, 2011: 20)

Try this As you were growing up, your parents and/or carers no doubt used some phrases that you remember well. You may remember them as, 'X always used to say ... when I was little/young.' A very common example would be something like, 'Work hard at school and you'll get a good job.' Think back and write down some examples of these. How have these phrases influenced your personal values?

Reflecting with others

This section will:

- Discuss what makes good supervision
- Introduce you to a model for supervision
- Help you to engage effectively with supervision
  - Introduce you to the concept of the reflective conversation

What is good supervision?

When examining a particular term, it is usually helpful to start with a definition of it. However, in relation to supervision this is difficult, because how it is defined will depend on the particular professional context. This means that it will be important to check the meaning of supervision within your particular work setting. It is important to emphasise that the kind of supervision we are discussing here should not be confused with that usually provided by your line manager, which tends to focus on the achievement (or otherwise) of set goals and targets. One big issue within the literature on supervision is whether or not it should be provided by a practitioner's manager. Some professions would argue that this should not be the case, whilst others would argue that it can be helpful. In some circumstances there is simply no choice.

The overall purpose of supervision is to encourage professionals to reflect on their practice in a deeper way in order to enhance their professional development. This is shown in the diagram below.

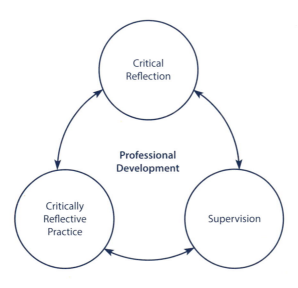

Figure 6 Professional development and supervision

So far, the main emphasis within this journal has been on reflection as an individual activity. Whilst this is very important, there is no doubt that much can be learned from reflecting with others. This process gives us vital feedback in relation to our development and enables us to see things that we simply would not see otherwise (see Theme 5). It is also important to note that supervision is not always open to everyone who feels they need it or feels they would benefit from it. In the early days of a new job, it is good to check out the opportunities for supervision and to consider making use of them wherever possible.

Like many other areas of professional practice, we cannot assume that all supervision is good supervision. In many respects, good supervisors have lots of the qualities of good teachers and good practitioners. They show respect for those they are supervising and demonstrate empathy. They often take a questioning approach as distinct from a didactic one and have excellent listening skills. A sense of humour is important too. It is good to remember that supervisors need feedback too, and giving this in a positive way can help to cement and maintain a healthy working relationship.

'Reflective thinking means suspending our judgement until we have carried out some sort of systematic enquiry.'

(Campbell and Norton, 2007: 141)

Models of supervision

There are many theoretical models that explore and explain the concept of supervision and one of the most well known is that of Proctor (1986). Proctor uses the following three terms to describe the functions of supervision.

- **Normative** – this involves monitoring the work of the practitioner to ensure that they are practising effectively in ways that are competent and ethical. This includes checking that the relevant code of ethical practice is being applied consistently and appropriately. The main question being posed here is: 'Is the practitioner meeting the norms of the particular profession?'
- **Formative** – the focus here is on the practitioner's professional development and the aim is to help them to develop their skills, professional knowledge, and appropriate attitudes and values. This leads to a greater and deeper level of self-awareness. The question being posed here is: 'How can this practitioner develop themselves further?'
- **Restorative** – this is sometimes referred to as supportive and is concerned with the support practitioners need when faced with challenging situations. Such situations cause stress and sometimes distress and it is important that practitioners have an opportunity to process their emotional responses (see Theme 6). In extreme cases, failing to do so could result in burn-out. The question being posed here is: 'How can this practitioner be supported in processing their thoughts and feelings in relation to challenging situations?'

Effective supervision can only happen in a safe space and supervisors and supervisees have a responsibility to be sure that the circumstances for supervision enable it to take place comfortably and without interruption. A high level of trust between supervisor and supervisee is vital, whist observing the general principles of confidentiality – that nothing should be disclosed to another party without the permission of the discloser, unless they are at risk of harm or are violating the law. It is also important to note that supervision protects clients, too, in ensuring that practitioners are competent (normative), professional (formative) and able to cope with stressful situations (restorative).

Try this Think about what you would like to gain from your next supervision session using Proctor's (1986) three headings Normative, Formative and Restorative. If you do not have access to supervision, think about how you might be able to access some support from others, again under Proctor's headings.

How to engage effectively with supervision

Supervision can offer a vital opportunity for critical reflection and it is important to think about how you can engage with the process in order to gain the maximum amount from it. The following points are worth thinking about at the start of the supervision process and before each session.

In order to benefit from supervision, it is important to think about what you hope to gain from it. Before a supervision session it is always good to spend some time in preparation. Going into a session without thinking it through first could mean that you gain little from it and you could also give the impression that you are not taking it seriously. Understandably this can make supervisors unhappy! Make sure that you are clear about anything that your supervisor has asked you to prepare or think about beforehand.

Effective supervisors usually make explicit ground rules with their supervisees at the beginning of their relationship and you should expect to make a contribution to establishing these. Beforehand, think about how you would like to work with your supervisor, including when, where and how often you would like to meet, as well as what your expectations are from supervision. These ground rules provide helpful boundaries to the supervisory relationship. Be prepared to be open and to reflect on your beliefs and values. Any kind of self-disclosure is a choice (see Theme 5) and an effective supervisor will offer a safe space where you can feel free to take some risks, such as disclosing things without the fear of ridicule. The usual protocols around confidentiality will apply.

When writing about supervision, Reid and Westergaard (2013) argue that it is a parallel process. This means that some of the interpersonal skills used in professional practice (such as empathy, congruence or genuineness and active listening) are mirrored in the supervision session by both parties. Remember that supervision is generally recognised as an important process for people in the helping professions and that through it your practice will be enriched and your stress levels reduced.

Try this   Think about how you can gain the most from supervision. Are there any barriers or constraints that you experience? If so, how could these be minimised?

The reflective conversation

We have established that reflection is not always a solitary activity and there are times when reflecting with others can be very helpful. Ghaye (2011) discusses the value of the reflective conversation as an aid to critical reflection on professional practice. With its theoretical roots in positive psychology, at the heart of the conversation is the desire to reflect constructively, creatively and critically, particularly in relation to the values that underpin practice. In a reflective conversation, these values should be questioned closely (Ghaye uses the word 'interrogated' here), in order to enable the practitioner to see if they can be justified or not within this particular context. If not, they will need to be reinterpreted.

'When all is chaos around me and I can only see and dwell on what is going wrong, there may be others able to see what is going well.'

Ghaye makes the following points about the reflective conversation:

- It should always include a discussion of values
- It can start as a conversation with yourself, but should then progress to a conversation held between two people
- It often has a question and response format – it is a dialogical process
- It should not just focus on the past, but should also consider the future
- Space and time needs to be set aside for the conversation
- It helps practitioners to make sense of experience and to build collaborative knowledge
- It is based on experience which happens in a social context
- It can lead to enlightenment and empowerment and can add meaning to what we know already.

Reflective conversations have much in common with supervision sessions and involve an understanding of the ground rules, active listening and empathy.

Examples of questions that can be asked in a conversation are:

- What is my professional work like and what values do I bring to it?
- What is successful about my work?
- What evidence do I have for its success?
- How has my work come to be successful?
- What is the effect of my work on my clients?
- What do I need to improve and how can I achieve this?

Remember that it is important to think about who you have a reflective conversation with; a critical friend will often be a good starting point.

'Above all else, a
reflective conversation is
one that involves a discussion of
values.'

(Ghaye and Ghaye, 1998: 19)

Try this   Try having a reflective conversation with your critical friend or supervisor using the questions in Theme 9.4. Following the discussion think about how useful this was. What did you feel you gained from it? How difficult was this and what were the challenges?

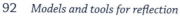

Bringing it all together and moving forward

This section will:

- Introduce you to the Integrated Reflective Cycle

  - Discuss two seminal theories in relation to the management of change

    - Introduce you to Johns' work on reflection as a way of being

      - Encourage you to engage in Senge's Personal Mastery

The Integrated Reflective Cycle

In this journal, we have examined a range of theoretical approaches and practical issues in relation to reflective practice. We began our journey with an exploration of some seminal literature on reflective practice, which encourages us to learn from our professional experience by evaluating it, in order to improve it. We then progressed towards our destination of critically reflective practice by examining the role of feelings in relation to professional practice, followed by a consideration of how we make assumptions and the importance of challenging these in order to practise in a critically reflective way. To do this, the importance of considering our own ethics and values was discussed and the importance of reflecting with others was highlighted as part of this process.

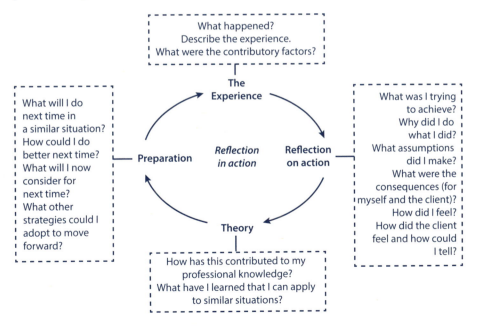

Figure 7 *The Integrated Reflective Cycle*

The Integrated Reflective Cycle (Bassot, 2012) shown in Figure 7 draws on several of these approaches. It is useful to compare and contrast different theories, as they often have their relative strengths and weaknesses. In this cycle, I highlight the strengths of a number of theoretical models and have posed questions around the cycle in order to prompt your thinking. Taking a questioning approach to your professional practice is an excellent way of delving deeper into not only what you did, but why – a key feature of critically reflective practice. Clearly, this approach is not completely new as this cycle draws on some of the questions posed by Gibbs (1998) and Johns (2009).

Like any other model, the Integrated Reflective Cycle needs to be critiqued as it also has its strengths and weaknesses. Critiquing theory and, in particular, its relationship to professional practice is always necessary. Its strengths are the things that will allow you to take your practice forward and its weaknesses are the aspects that could hinder your progress, which therefore need to be discarded. However, it is always important to be clear about the reasons for your critique and to make sure that you can justify these. For example, focusing on a model just because you like it may not be a position you can easily defend. Equally, discarding something just because it takes you into difficult territory is also questionable. Critically reflective practice demands that we accept a level of 'inner discomfort' (Boyd and Fales, 1983: 106) to enable our practice to develop.

'Reflective practice leads
to more searching questions,
the opening of fascinating avenues to
explore, but few secure answers.'

(Bolton, 2005: 24)

Managing change

Engaging in professional development always involves coping with a level of change in relation to several different aspects of life, both personal and professional. It is often helpful to take an analytical approach to help you to understand more about how you approach change and cope with it. Lewin developed two very useful theories that serve as analytical tools in relation to understanding how change can be managed.

In his force field analysis, Lewin (1951) used a scientific approach which he applied to social situations. He argued that there are forces that promote change (driving forces) and those that work against it (restraining forces). An issue or situation is held in balance by the interaction between the two forces. Lewin calls this balance 'quasi stationary equilibrium', which represents the present state. In order for change to happen and to achieve movement towards what Lewin calls the desired state, either the driving forces need to be maximised or the restraining forces need to be minimised. When both happen together the amount of change is greatest.

'My work life is a work in progress.'

Linked with these ideas, Lewin (1951) also developed his three-step model, which is as follows:

- **Step 1** – Unfreezing, which involves reducing the restraining factors
- **Step 2** – Movement, or encouraging the development of new ideas and practices focusing on the driving forces
- **Step 3** – Refreezing, stabilising the changes at the new level of 'quasi stationary equilibrium' to avoid slipping back into old practices.

Lewin's models are very helpful tools for analysing your own responses to change, but also those of your colleagues and clients. Whether these can be applied in their entirety today is questionable. For example, his concept of refreezing could suggest the kind of stability that our fast-paced and ever-changing world never appears to have. However, many argue that Lewin's theories have become seminal in the field of organisational behaviour. Bringing them into the theoretical arena of critically reflective practice so as to understand processes of change is also helpful.

Try this   Think about a period of change that you have either experienced recently or that you are about to experience. Describe the driving forces for change and the restraining forces. Evaluate how easy or difficult the change was or will be in relation to these forces.

From 'doing reflection' to 'reflection as a way of being'

In his book *Becoming a Reflective Practitioner*, Johns (2004) examines five different levels of reflection, moving from 'doing reflection' at a surface level to 'reflection as a way of being' at the deepest level.

1   The first level is described as 'reflection-on-experience' where the practitioner reflects on an experience after the event in order to gain insights that might inform their future practice. This is a reminder of Schön's (1983) reflection on action (Theme 4) and Kolb's (1984) cycle (Theme 3).

2   The second level is Johns' 'reflection-in-action', which he describes as pausing during an experience in order to make sense of it, leading to reframing the situation in order to move towards a desired outcome, for example by trying a different strategy.

3   The third level is termed 'the internal supervisor', which involves the practitioner having a dialogue with themselves while they are interacting with another person, again in order to make sense of the situation. This could take the form of a questioning approach with yourself.

4   The fourth level is 'reflection-within-the-moment' and demands that the practitioner has an awareness of how they are thinking, feeling and responding as an event is unfolding. Importantly this includes being open to changing or shifting your views and ideas as you practice.

5   The fifth and deepest level is 'mindful practice', where the practitioner has a high level of awareness of self and what they desire from their practice. This links with Senge's (2006) ideas of vision, which will be discussed in the next section.

In his later edition published in 2009, Johns' understanding of mindfulness has developed, keeping the idea of achieving desirable practice as the aim but also involving what he describes as 'seeing things as they really are' and 'without distortion' (p. 10). Such a statement is always open to critique, in that it is questionable whether this is achievable or not. It is, however, something to aim for.

In reviewing the journey we have taken so far in this journal, from reflective practice to critically reflective practice, it could be argued that we began at the first level of Johns' model and are now considering aspects of 'mindfulness' at the deepest level.

Theme 10.4 Senge's Personal Mastery

In his book *The Fifth Discipline*, Senge (2006) discusses his concept of Personal Mastery, which involves living life from a creative viewpoint rather than a reactive one. To engage in Personal Mastery, we need to clarify continually what is important to us and where we want to be as practitioners (our vision) and learn to see our current reality more clearly. Imagine stretching an elastic band between your two hands, one hand above the other. The hand above is your vision; this can be summed up as the kind of practitioner you would like to be. The lower hand is your current reality. The elastic band stretched between the two represents the creative tension between your vision and your current reality. This creative tension is central to Senge's concept of Personal Mastery.

Tension is a word that often has negative connotations associated with stress and distress. Creative tension, however, is a positive concept and needs to be harnessed. Creative tension is the source of the creative energy that we need in order to continue learning and developing. It enables our practice to keep moving forward and is vital in retaining a high level of motivation and commitment to professional practice.

'To remember where you come from is in part to know where you're going.'

In the image of the elastic band outlined above, there are, of course, two things that can happen as the tension is released. Either the hand below moves towards the hand above – so I keep my vision and my current reality moves towards it. Or the hand above moves down towards the hand below as I lose sight of my vision and it moves towards the acceptance of my current reality. It is important to note that as my current reality moves towards my vision, my vision must continue to move forward (upwards) in order to maintain the creative tension. People who show a high level of Personal Mastery continually reappraise their vision, in order to maintain the creative tension needed to propel themselves forward through a continuous process of learning.

Although we have now reached the end of our ten themes, the work of Senge urges us to continue developing through renewing our vision in order to protect and foster our creative tension.

'I pay attention
to my "experience" because
I constantly strive to become a more
effective practitioner and realise my
vision of practice.'

(Johns, 2004: 6)

Try this Imagine you overhear a group of friends and/or colleagues describing you and your work. Write down what you hope they would be saying. Now use this as the basis for writing your vision for your practice. Now think of some examples of how you can make progress towards your vision.

Part 2

More space for
reflection

Activities

Part 2 offers
you more space for
reflective writing and contains
a number of activities and quotes to
help inspire you. The activities are designed
to help you to continue to reflect critically on
your learning and development. The quotes offer
insights from a number of writers into different
aspects of reflection, like the quotes in Part 1. How
you use these pages is up to you and you should feel
free to use them as suits you best at the time.

Remember to date your writing for the following
two reasons; first, it is very easy to forget when
things happened and, second, it is good
to look back and see how your work is
developing over time.

Try this Many writers use metaphors as a helpful way of explaining abstract concepts. Thompson (2005) describes the concept of reflective practice by using the metaphor of bespoke tailoring. Imagine you are attending a very special event and you have enough money to buy your ideal outfit. You know exactly what you want but cannot see it in the shops. So you decide to go to a bespoke tailor or dressmaker and ask them to make it for you. What processes will they go through to ensure that you get the outfit of your dreams? Where are the parallels between this and working with people in a reflective way?

'Maybe just being aware that my assumptions could be wrong and unhelpful is a good start.'

More space for reflection

'Reflective
practice involves
cutting the cloth to suit
the specific circumstances,
rather than looking for ready-made
solutions.'

(Thompson, 2005: 196)

Try this Brookfield (1995) suggests that there are four lenses through which we can reflect on practice critically. They are as follows:

1 Our own autobiographies and experiences as learners
2 The eyes of our clients
3 The experiences of our colleagues
4 Theoretical literature

Think about how each of these lenses will give you a different perspective on your practice and bear in mind issues of power in the helping relationship. Now think of times when you have engaged in critical reflection using each of the four lenses. Are there any of the four that you are reluctant to use? Why might this be? Does this need to change? If so, how? If not, why not?

'Every
situation is
different and requires
its own unique way of
dealing with it.'

More space for reflection

'What frame of
reference (or lens) is being
used to make sense of what has happened?
What theories are being applied to this situation?
It is easy to reinforce previously held opinions about
people and situations which may lead to prejudice and
discriminatory practice, if we do not recognise what we
are using to make sense of reflections.'

(Knott and Scragg, 2010: 6)

Try this The most common reason that practitioners give for not engaging in reflective practice is lack of time. Most professionals work in busy environments where the pace is fast and there is usually too much to do. In such circumstances, it can be tempting to switch on your 'auto pilot' and rely on what you already know in order to cope with the workload.

Working from the premise that we do not have any 'free' time at work – the only time we have is the time we make – why is it important to make time to reflect? Now write down how you could put this into practice.

Having some physical space for reflection can also be very important. Describe your ideal space – what would it look like and where would it be? How else can you gain some space for reflection?

'Rather than acting
or responding, I am now taking
a moment to reflect in action and refer back to
similar experiences. This approach allows me to think on
my feet as I am drawing on prior experiences. It means
that I am now able to adapt my behaviour in order
to gain a more positive outcome.'

More space for reflection

'All professionals are
concerned with knowing
and realising desirable and effective
practice, yet work in conditions
where for one reason or another such
realisation is often difficult.'

(Johns, 2009, p. xi)

Try this Think of an example from your practice where you have begun to think about something differently. Now try describing how this change came about on one side of the page and how your assumptions were challenged on the other side.

'Reflection gives me a
sense of relief, a way to look over a
situation, revisit it in a time and place that is
relaxed and with a more open mind without
distraction.'

Critical reflection 'happens when we identify and scrutinise the assumptions that undergird how we work.'

(Brookfield, 1995: xii)

Try this Think about your development over the past few months. Now try to depict this visually – for example as a diagram, graph or picture. Remember that you do not have to be artistic to be able to do this, as a simple line drawing can be very effective.

'Studying
reflective practice has
really had a major impact
on my life. I am already much
more self-aware.'

More space for reflection

'Reflective practice
is very important for a
number of reasons. Chief amongst these
is the significance of linking theory to practice –
that is, making sure that our actions are drawing on
a professional knowledge base and not simply on
guesswork or ill-informed assumptions.'

(Thompson, 2009: 65)

Try this   Now look at the picture, diagram or graph from page 122 and try writing a story about what it depicts.

'Writing in my journal is
a big help. If I have something
going round in my head, I now write it
down, it feels like it gets it out there and I
can either leave it there, or do something
about it.'

'Critically reflective practice
can play a crucial part in trying
to make sure that professional practice
is geared towards positive, emancipatory
outcomes, rather than reinforcing patterns of
inequality and disadvantage.'

(Thompson and Thompson, 2008: 30)

Try this Find a photograph or image that depicts how you feel about your progress at the moment. Now describe it and try to summarise what it means for you.

'I am beginning
to realise that I do reflect
a great deal. However, the process
of writing in my journal is making me
think more about how I acted and whether
this was the best method in such
circumstances.'

Reflective practice involves taking 'a dual stance, being on the one hand, the actor in a drama and on the other hand, the critic who sits in the audience watching and analysing the entire performance.'

(Osterman and Kottkamp, 2004: 23)

Try this Knott and Scragg (2011) suggest looking back over a number of diary entries to see if there are any key themes emerging over time. This can help you to highlight some specific areas you would like to work on. Now have a look through what you have written in this journal. Are any particular themes emerging? What would you now like to work on?

'At first I was a bit uncertain
about how I would manage reflecting in
writing. It felt strange to write my thoughts, I was
happy to think behind closed doors in my own mind
but felt slightly exposed putting pen to paper.'

'Becoming mindful
… the antidote to
complacency, habit and
blindness.'

(Johns, 2004: 5)

Try this Write a letter to a friend or someone you know well discussing the highs and lows of your recent experiences. You could save this and post it to yourself in a few months time to examine how you have progressed since then.

'I realise that
I have more to gain
as a practitioner if I analyse my
experience and understand the meanings
behind my action and whether I could
have acted differently.'

'Reflective practice
helps us to question our
assumptions and prevents us from accepting
things at face value. It encourages a deeper
examination of issues, which is particularly necessary
when promoting equality and social justice for clients.'

(Reid and Bassot, 2011: 107)

Try this   Try writing a SWOT (strengths, weaknesses, opportunities and threats) analysis of your learning and development. How can you build on your strengths, address your weaknesses, take full advantage of the opportunities and work to minimise the threats?

'My patience has
been pushed to the limit both
personally and professionally, but having
the reflective journal to unload my thoughts into
helps me to have some positivity that I can resolve
today's situations with positive results for
all concerned.'

'The word "competent"
can be problematic, as it may
imply that the practitioner is "good
enough". Many practitioners wish to strive
for excellence, and reflective practice offers one
key means by which this can be achieved.'

(Reid and Bassot, 2011: 107)

More space for reflection

More space for reflection

Part 3

Career development

Part 3 offers
you the opportunity to
look forward and focus on your
career development. It is important
to understand that the world of work is
changing at a rapid rate, and that this brings
challenges to people in all areas of the labour
market as they recognise the need to think
about career differently. The Career Learning and
Development (CLD) Bridge model is introduced as
a means of illustrating this, followed by a number
of activities to help you to work towards career
happiness, build career resilience and establish
career growth.

Career development

In Part 3 we start to look forward and move on to examine some relevant career development issues. You may have already made some career decisions or you may still be unsure about what you want to do in the future. Equally, you may currently be working and thinking about your next career move. Whatever your situation, it is useful to consider your present position and where you might like to be in the future. This could relate to your medium and longer term goals (if you are clear about them), or it could mean trying to establish some. We begin by examining some of the ways that the world of work is changing and the challenges this brings to people in all areas of the labour market. This is followed by a brief introduction to the Career Learning and Development (CLD) Bridge model which explains some of the factors involved in how people make their career decisions. This is followed by a number of activities that you can carry out in order to think about your own career development.

In all situations – whether you are on a professional course of study, are already working in a professional context, or simply beginning to think about your future – it will be very useful to keep a record of your learning and development. This will be particularly helpful when you apply for jobs in the future. It is easy to think that we will remember what we have done, but in reality we often do not. This means that we can waste a lot of time trying to remember the detail and looking back to get accurate dates for when we did certain things. Part 3 also acts as a record of your learning and development and is likely to save you time in the future, whilst also giving you an opportunity to reflect on your experiences at work or on placement.

Change and career

There is no doubt that the world is changing at a rapid pace, particularly in response to the impact of such things as ICT and globalised marketplaces. In the past, the term 'career' was seen as an occupation, or some kind of paid work, which also implied an element of progression. It was something tangible that someone could find by analysing themselves (for example, their interests and skills) and the opportunities available to try and get the closest match. Having found a good match, they could then work to make progress within their chosen area. This view of 'career' was very helpful when times were stable and to a large extent predictable. However, more recently the idea of 'a job for life' has come into question and many have begun to see 'career' as a metaphorical journey through life, moving from one area of work to the next – sometimes with breaks in between. In addition, 'career' is now often seen in terms of life as a whole, not just paid work, as issues such as work/life balance become more important.

Many aspects of our lives are changing, not just the world of work, and everyone needs to embrace change in order to progress – some might say in order to survive. This means engaging in lifelong learning to update your knowledge and skills on a continuous basis. In recent years the notion of 'employment', with its connotations of security and progression, is frequently being replaced by the idea of 'employability'. The onus is shifting onto individuals to make themselves as employable as possible. This usually means being prepared to engage in training and development, to respond appropriately as the needs of employers change, and to be prepared for the consequences of being part of companies and organisations that need to downsize or rebrand themselves in times of recession and budget cuts. Flexibility and employability therefore go 'hand in hand'. However, this does not necessarily mean that the notion of a career for life is dead, but rather that we all need to be as well prepared as possible for the challenges that change brings.

Career as a journey

The idea of career as a journey can be very helpful, particularly for those people who do not yet know what they want to do. Looking a long way ahead is often difficult, particularly when we live in an unpredictable world. Rather than trying to answer the age-old question, 'What do I want to do with the rest of my life?', many people find it easier to focus on the next step. Even looking a few years ahead can be daunting for some and the classic interview question, 'Where do you see yourself in five years' time?' is notoriously difficult to answer – many interviewers themselves would struggle to respond to it! Whether you are someone who has medium- or even long-term goals or whether you are very uncertain about the future, focusing on the next step will help you to make progress in your career thinking.

The Career Learning and Development Bridge

In my recent work (Bassot, 2009), I have developed the Career Learning and Development (CLD) Bridge as a way of explaining the concepts of career and career development in more detail. (See Figure 8 overleaf.) The CLD Bridge uses the metaphor of a suspension bridge. Suspension bridges function because the tension in the cables, compression in the towers, and the weight of the road are all kept in balance. Without this balance, they would collapse. I chose the metaphor of a suspension bridge because it illustrates the tensions that many people experience between what they want as individuals and the demands of their context. The Bridge harnesses these tensions and relies on them in order to function, showing that in relation to career, tensions and stress can be seen as opportunities and possibilities rather than threats, without underestimating the many challenges that are involved.

Taking account of the constant and rapid changes in the world at large, the CLD Bridge operates with two-way traffic. It is important to understand that you do not cross the Bridge once, but travel back and forth across it as your career develops. This illustrates the need to engage in continuous professional development, in order to meet your own needs and those of your employers. Career, then, is something that you construct throughout your life and is not a 'one-off' decision. To many, this will be a relief, as the idea of making a decision (or, worse, a mistake) that determines one's career for the rest of one's life is a daunting prospect.

We will now focus on the three aspects of the bridge that are highlighted in the diagram.

First, on the left-hand side is career happiness. Career happiness is focused on what you want as an individual and can include such things as maintaining a healthy work/life balance and choosing a field of work where you will gain satisfaction. This often involves making choices that are in tune with your values, which can affect the sector that you choose to work in (for example,

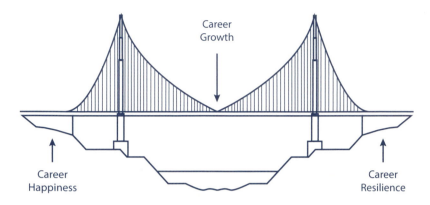

Figure 8 The Career Learning and Development Bridge

corporate, public, charity). These values can be extrinsic (such as the importance of earning a high salary), intrinsic (such as feeling respected for what I do and making a difference), or lifestyle values (such as where I live and how far I will have to travel to work), or any combination of these.

Second, and on the right-hand side of the Bridge, is career resilience. This is vital in enabling you to cope in the changing world and its turbulent labour market. Career resilience means being positive about challenges and being able to 'bounce back' from disappointments. It involves developing a strong underlying belief in yourself, including your knowledge and your skills, by focusing on positive feedback and working on your development points. Having a high level of self-reliance is also important in building career resilience, as is being receptive to change rather than fighting against it or dismissing it.

The road represents career growth (Bassot, Barnes and Chant, forthcoming) and is based on Vygotsky's (1978) concept of the Zone of Proximal Development (ZPD). Wood (1998, p. 26) defines the ZPD as 'the gap that exists for an individual child (or adult) between what he is able to do alone, and what he (*sic*) can achieve with help from one more knowledgeable than himself'. The focus of learning and development in the ZPD is on what a person is able to do next rather than what lies far ahead in the distance. In relation to career, you can make progress within the ZPD by gaining useful practical experience and by having discussions with others who are more knowledgeable (for example, employers and careers advisers). These activities and discussions enable you to write (in a metaphorical sense) your career narrative, or story.

The following activities are designed to help you to think about how you can work towards career happiness, develop career resilience and maintain career growth.

Try this Describe the times in the past when you felt happiest. Try and identify some of the reasons that made you happy at those times. Make a list of the things that will make you happy in the future. Is there anything surprising here?

Try this What does the term 'job satisfaction' mean to you? Make a list of the things that are vital for you when you think about a job or career that will give you satisfaction. Now rank them in order of importance. In light of what you have written, how would you describe your core values in relation to your career development?

Try this How would a good friend describe you as a person? How would you describe yourself? Are there any differences?

Try this   This activity is about career resilience. Describe your core skills under the following headings. Use the right-hand column to note things you need to work on – be as honest as you can. This process will be helpful when you need to write a personal statement as part of a job application.

Table 1 Core skills and development points

Core Skills	Development Points
Communication – oral With individuals With groups In meetings Other **Communication – written** Reports Case notes Course assignments Other	
Communication – ICT Managing e-mails Word processing Spreadsheets Other Numeracy Budgets Expenses Keeping relevant statistics Other	
Team work – your role in a team	
Leadership skills	
Problem solving	
Analytical skills	

Core Skills	Development Points
Organisational skills	
Creativity	
Resilience	

Now write a paragraph to summarise:

- Your strengths
- Your areas for development

Try this   Think about times when you have needed to overcome some difficulties. What strategies did you use at the time? What was successful and not successful?

Table 2 Log for work/placement experiences

Dates	Place/organisation	Contact details	Experience gained

Table 3 Training courses attended

Dates	Name of course	Place	Documents (certificates, attendance records)

Spend some time thinking about how you got to where you are now. Here are some questions that can help to guide you in developing your career narrative:

- Where am I now?
- How did I get here?
- Why did I choose to do what I am doing now?
- How did I make my decisions?

Rank your decisions using the following scale:

     5 = Excellent
     4 = Good
     3 = OK
     2 = Not good
     1 = Not good at all

What does this show you about how you have made your decisions and how you might make them in the future?

Try this   Imagine you are telling your career story so far to a friend. What would you include? Describe the most significant parts of your story so far.

Try this   Imagine it is 3 / 5 / 10 years from now. Where (generally) do you
hope to be and what will you have achieved?

1   Make a list of things about yourself that you feel have changed over the
    years.
2   Now list some things that have remained the same.
3   What do these things say about you as a person?
4   What kind of pointers do they give you in relation to your career
    development? This might include the insights they give you into the kind
    of person you are, the kind of work you might find satisfying and the kinds
    of things that could be important (even vital) to you in a job.

Annotated further reading

Many books have been written on the subject of reflective practice and most have been written for particular academic disciplines. Surprisingly few have been written for a general audience. Understandably tutors tend to recommend books from their own discipline and it is useful to follow their particular recommendations provided via reading lists. However, there might also be very useful texts beyond this, sometimes from another academic discipline or from texts written for a wider audience.

I have selected eight books to review here for those of you who would like to undertake some further reading. I have chosen them either because they are written for everyone who is interested in reflective practice, or because, even though they have been written for a particular sector, their content can easily be applied to others. In such cases, when reading them you need to remember not to be put off by any terminology that is not appropriate to your context and to replace it with the relevant terms from your own professional sphere in order to engage with the work. There is often much to be gained by reading work designed for a sector outside your own, particularly if your work demands that you work in an inter-professional way. I have selected books from a range of academic and professional disciplines and have focused on more recent publications as reviews on earlier texts can usually be found elsewhere. I have reviewed the books in alphabetical order by the author's or authors' surname(s) rather than ranking them in any order of preference. You will find the full reference for each of these books in the list of references at the end of the journal.

Reflective Practice in Counselling and Psychotherapy by *Sophie Bager-Charleson (2010)*

This is a very accessible book which in the early parts contains useful discussions of some of the key concepts introduced in this journal; for example, Schön's reflection on and in action, espoused theories and theories in use, and double-loop learning. The inextricable link between issues of change and loss are usefully highlighted in relation to work with clients.

In particular, the ABC model (p. 148) could be a very useful tool for your own reflections as well as for use during your work with clients. Schön's reflective contract (p. 51) is also worthy of some careful consideration regarding the differences between being an expert and being a reflective practitioner. Throughout the book there are clear chapter summaries, boxes with case studies, key thinkers, activities and reflection points. Whilst most of this content is written specifically for the context of counselling, some very familiar names and concepts appear that cross over into lots of other disciplines (for example, Foucault, postmodernism, social constructionism, narratives). The book concludes with a chapter on research where the ACT model is outlined, which could be applied to qualitative research across academic disciplines.

Reflective Practice: Writing and Professional Development by Gillie Bolton
(3rd edition, 2010)
If you have become interested in reflective writing through using this journal and want to examine this whole area in much more depth, you could find this book very useful. It includes some clear explanations of key complex terms, such as reflexivity, mindfulness and truth. The book is written for a wide audience and the author carefully uses the terms patients, students and clients throughout in order to emphasise this. Taking the metaphor of the mirror further, she uses the 'through the mirror' approach in relation to exploring uncertainties, playfulness (which requires being willing to experiment), and the kind of questioning that results in yet more questions that need to be posed. A recurring theme is 'write to learn' and Chapter 9 of the book gives a wide range of methods to show how this can be done. This is followed by three chapters on specific writing techniques – narrative, metaphor and a chapter on what the author describes as forms of writing that enable you to write 'wider and deeper'. In fitting style, the book concludes with a chapter entitled 'Reflection on reflection', emphasising the continuing nature of the reflective journey where an ultimate destination is never reached, but only stopping points along the way.

Reflective Practice in Nursing *edited by Chris Bulman and Sue Schutz (5th edition, 2013)*
As its title suggests, this book is written specifically for nurses, and people in this sector may well want to read this practical book in its entirety. For people in other professional arenas outside health, the following chapters are particularly useful. Chapter 1 by Bulman introduces readers to a very wide range of important writers on the whole subject of reflection. Chapter 2 by Atkins and Schutz, 'Developing skills for reflective practice', contains some very useful discussions on key terms, such as self-awareness, description, critical analysis, synthesis and evaluation. This particular chapter also includes individual reflective exercises and ones to do with a partner or a group, as well as 'thinking activities'. Chapter 8 by Schutz outlines some of the different ways that reflection can be assessed – in particular, it contains some very useful descriptions of such things as critical incident analysis, the reflective essay, the reflective case study and reflective journals. These will help students who need to submit pieces of work like this as part of their course of study. The book concludes with a very good chapter on getting started – for many readers this would seem to be the logical place to start reading.

Teaching and Learning through Reflective Practice: A Practical Guide for Positive Action *by Tony Ghaye (2nd edition, 2011)*
I chose this particular book because it is markedly different from many other books on the subject of reflective practice. Its roots are in positive psychology and as such it offers a healthy antidote from perspectives that focus purely on problems – or deficit models as they are referred to here. The author argues that a strengths-based approach can help professionals to understand and even transform their practice, whilst building resilience, remaining well motivated and feeling positive about their work. This is discussed in some detail in Chapter 4 which also includes a very useful exercise on discovering your strengths as well as an examination of how strengths can become weaknesses when they are overemphasised. An alternative model for supervision called the reflective conversation is put forward in Chapter 3 where some strengths-based questions are contrasted with some deficit-based ones. Chapter 5 focuses on 'reflection-on-values' and is particularly useful as it encourages us to examine

our own values and their origins and those of our particular profession. This is followed by some practical suggestions that can help us live out our values, including living by your word and promising less and doing more. The book concludes by encouraging us to build a 'desire to think again'.

Becoming a Reflective Practitioner *by Christopher Johns (3rd edition, 2009)*
If you are serious about taking a deeply reflective approach to your work, you may well find this book inspiring – but it is not a book for the faint-hearted. Based on his vast experience of nursing, particularly in providing alternative therapies in hospices, the author begins by laying the foundations for the book in the first chapter. Here he puts forward a typology of reflective practice with five levels from 'doing reflection' to 'reflection as a way of being'. He argues that the prerequisites for this are such things as openness, curiosity and commitment as well as energy and passion. The chapters that follow examine a wide range of issues that are clearly pertinent to the health sector, but are written in such a way as to make them accessible to a wide range of readers. Indeed, reading them will provide insights into this world for those of us who do not have such experiences in our working lives. In particular, Chapter 15 on transformational leadership makes vital connections between reflective practice and creating better environments for others. Throughout the book the author uses examples drawn from practice (like scripts and case notes) to illustrate the points he is making. These bring the book alive and make it both easy to read and for some, difficult to put down.

Learning Journals: A Handbook for Reflective Practice and Professional development *by Jennifer Moon (2nd edition, 2006)*
This is a comprehensive book which examines in detail many different aspects of learning journals and is written for a wide audience. As an avid journal writer herself, the author explores a range of issues in relation to how people learn from journal writing, how journals can be used and their link with personal and professional development. Chapter 9 contains helpful advice on how to start writing a journal and the final chapter offers a very wide range of activities to enhance journal writing, such as concept mapping and writing from different perspectives. The book concludes with examples of reflective writing which could be very helpful for those who are new to the process.

Critical Reflection in Practice: Generating Knowledge for Care *by Gary
Rolfe, Melanie Jasper and Dawn Freshwater (2nd edition, 2011)*
This is a very comprehensive book written for people in healthcare
professions. In the first two chapters a wide range of theory is introduced to
help readers begin to engage with critical reflection. The content is illustrated
with useful diagrams and tables along with clear examples to show the
relevant theory being applied in practice. The authors then proceed to discuss
a range of relevant topics such as reflective writing, supervision (individual
and in groups) and using reflection in research. Throughout the book there
are 'reflective moments' where the authors encourage and challenge readers
to think through situations they have encountered. These are written in an
informal style and could be used by individuals, pairs or groups.

The Critically Reflective Practitioner *by Sue Thompson and Neil Thompson
(2008)*
Although the background of the two authors is in social health and work,
this book is written generically and could be used by a wide range of people
in the helping professions. Its clear and succinct style and the layout make it
extremely accessible to readers. The authors show great skill in being able to
explain complex concepts and issues in an engaging way. This book also has a
refreshing emphasis throughout on the role of critical reflection in promoting
anti-discriminatory practice. Part 1 of the book focuses on understanding
reflective practice. The book starts with a useful section on what reflective
practice is not and from the beginning presents a strong argument for its
importance in professional practice. The authors introduce the concept
of 'reflection-for-action' which involves thinking ahead and planning for
what could happen. They also emphasise the need for theory and practice
to be integrated – theory informs practice and vice versa. The position of
the authors is that reflective practice is a duty and a responsibility at both
an individual and organisational level. Part 2 focuses on making reflective
practice happen and includes many helpful suggestions of tools and strategies
to promote reflection. The book concludes with a call to rise to the challenge
that critically reflective practice brings to make professional work effective,
rewarding and creative.

References

Adams, J., Hayes, J. and Hopson, B. (1976) *Transition: Understanding and Managing Personal Change*, London: Martin Robertson.

Argyris, C. (1982) *Reasoning, Learning and Action: Individual and Organizational*, San Francisco, CA: Jossey-Bass.

Argyris, C. and Schön, D. (1974) *Theory in Practice: Increasing Professional Effectiveness*, San Francisco, CA: Jossey-Bass.

Bager-Charleson, S. (2010) *Reflective Practice in Counselling and Psychotherapy,* Exeter: Learning Matters.

Bassot, B. (2009) 'Career Learning and Development: A bridge to the future', in H. L. Reid (ed.), *Constructing the Future: Career Guidance for Changing Contexts*, Stourbridge: Institute of Career Guidance.

Bassot, B. (2012) *The Reflective Diary*, Kibworth Beauchamp: Matador, n.p.

Bassot, B., Barnes, A. and Chant, A. (forthcoming) *A Practical Guide to Career Learning and Development: Innovation in Career Education 11–19*, London: Routledge.

Bolton, G. (2005) *Reflective Practice: Writing and Professional Development*, 2nd edn, London: Sage.

Bolton, G. (2010) *Reflective Practice: Writing and Professional Development*, 3rd edn, London: Sage.

Borton, T. (1970) *Reach, Touch and Teach*, London: McGraw-Hill.

Boud, D., Keogh, R. and Walker, D. (1985) *Reflection: Turning Experience into Learning*, London: RoutledgeFalmer.

Boyd, E. M. and Fales, A. W. (1983) 'Reflective learning: Key to learning from experience', *Journal of Humanistic Psychology*, 23.2: 99–117.

Brockbank, A. and McGill, I. (2006) *Facilitating Reflective Learning through Mentoring and Coaching*, London: Kogan Page.

Brookfield, S. D. (1995) *Becoming a Critically Reflective Teacher*, San Francisco, CA: Jossey-Bass.

Bulman, C. (2008) 'An introduction to reflection', in C. Bulman and S. Schutz (eds*)*, *Reflective Practice in Nursing*, 4th edn, Chichester: Wiley-Blackwell.

Bulman, C. and Schutz, S. (2013) *Reflective Practice in Nursing*, 5th edn, Oxford: Wiley-Blackwell.

Campbell, A. and Norton, L. (2007) *Learning Teaching and Assessing in Higher Education*, Exeter: Learning Matters.

Corey, G., Schneider Corey, M. and Callanan, P. (2007) *Issues and Ethics in the Helping Professions*, 7th edn, Belmont, CA: Thomson Brooks/Cole.

Covey, S. (2004) *The 7 Habits of Highly Effective People,* London: Pocket Books.

Driscoll, J. (2007) (ed.) *Practising Clinical Supervision: A Reflective Approach for Healthcare Professionals*, Edinburgh: Ballière Tindall, Elsevier.

Eraut, M. (1994) *Developing Professional Knowledge and Competence*, London: RoutledgeFalmer.

Eraut, M. (2006) 'Editorial', *Learning in Health and Social Care*, 5.3: 111–18.

Fook, J. (2004) 'Critical reflection and transformative possibilities', in L. Davies and P. Leonard (eds), *Social Work in a Corporate Era*, Aldershot: Ashgate.

Ghaye, T. (2011) *Teaching and Learning through Reflective Practice: A Practical Guide for Positive Action*, Abingdon: Routledge.

Ghaye, T. and Ghaye, K. (1998) *Teaching and Learning through Critical Reflective Practice*, London: Routledge David Fulton Press.

Gibbs, G. (1998) *Learning by Doing: A Guide to Teaching and Learning Methods*, Oxford: Further Education Unit, Oxford Polytechnic.

Honey, P (undated) *The Learning Styles Questionnaire*, online. Available at http://www.peterhoney.com/content/LearningStylesQuestionnaire.html (accessed 20 March 2012).

Honey, P. and Mumford, A. (2000) *The Learning Styles Helper's Guide*, Maidenhead: Peter Honey Publications.

Howatson-Jones, L. (2010) *Reflective Practice in Nursing*, Exeter: Learning Matters.

Jarvis, P. (1994) 'Learning practical knowledge', *Journal of Further and Higher Education*, 18.1: 31–43.

Jasper, M. (2003) *Beginning Reflective Practice*, Cheltenham: Nelson Thornes

Jasper, M. (2008) 'Using reflective journals and diaries to enhance practice and learning', in C. Bulman and S. Schutz (eds), *Reflective Practice in Nursing*, 4th edn, Chichester: Wiley-Blackwell.

Johns, C. (2004) *Becoming a Reflective Practitioner*, 2nd edn, Oxford: Blackwell Publishing.

Johns, C. (2009) *Becoming a Reflective Practitioner*, 3rd edn, Chichester: Wiley-Blackwell.

Johns, C. (2010) *Guided Reflection: A Narrative Approach to Advancing Professional Practice*, Oxford: Wiley-Blackwell.

Knott, C. and Scragg, T. (2011) *Reflective Practice in Social Work*, 2nd edn, Exeter: Learning Matters.

Knowles, G. and Lander, V. (2012) *Thinking through Ethics and Values in Primary Education*, London: Learning Matters.

Kolb, D. (1984) *Experiential Learning: Experience as the Source of Learning and Development*, New Jersey: Prentice Hall.

Lewin, K. (1951) *Field Theory in Social Science*, New York: Harper & Row.

Luft, H. (1984) *Group Processes, an Introduction to Group Dynamics*, Mountain View, CA: Mayfield.

Luzio, E. (2011) 'The Ladder of Inference Creates Bad Judgment', http://www.groupharmonics. com/HelpDesk/Ladder.htm (accessed 7 December 2012).

Mezirow, J. (1978) *Education for Perspective Transformation: Women's Re-entry Programs in Community Colleges*, New York: Center for Adult Education, Columbia University.

Mezirow, J. (1981) 'A critical theory of adult learning and education', *Adult Education*, 32.1: 13–24.

Moon, J. (2006) *Learning Journals: A Handbook for Reflective Practice and Professional Development*, 2nd edn, Abingdon: Routledge.

Osterman, K. F. and Kottkamp, R. B. (2004) *Reflective Practice for Educators*, 2nd edn, Thousand Oaks, CA: Corwin Press.

Proctor, B. (1986) 'Supervision: A co-operative exercise in accountability', in A. Marken and M. Payne (eds), *Enabling and Ensuring: Supervision in Practice*, Leicester: Leicester National Youth Bureau/Council for Education and Training in Youth and Community Work.

Reid, H. L. and Bassot, B. (2011) 'Reflection: A constructive space for career development', in M. McMahon and M. Watson (eds), *Career Counseling and Constructivism*, New York: Nova Science Publishers.

Reid, H. L. and Westergaard, J. (2013) *Effective Supervision for Counsellors: An Introduction*, Exeter: Learning Matters.

Riches, A. (2012) 'Where did that come from?' *How to Keep Control in any Situation*, e-book, Sudbury, MA: eBookIt. Available at http:// www.anneriches.com.au/almond-effect.html.

Rolfe, G., Jasper, M and Freshwater, D. (2011) *Critical Reflection in Practice*, 2nd edn, Basingstoke: Palgrave Macmillan.

Schön, D. A. (1983) *The Reflective Practitioner*, Aldershot: Ashgate.

Schön, D. A. (1987) *Educating the Reflective Practitioner*, San Francisco, CA: Jossey-Bass.

Senge, P. (2006) *The Fifth Discipline*, 2nd edn, London: Random House Business.

Thompson, N. (1995) *Theory and Practice in Health and Social Welfare*, Buckingham: Open University Press.

Thompson, N. (2005) 'Reflective Practice', in R. Harrison and C. Wise (eds), *Working with Young People*, London: Sage.

Thompson, N. (2009) *Practising Social Work*, Basingstoke: Palgrave Macmillan.

Thompson, N. (2012) *Anti-Discriminatory Practice*, 5th edn, Basingstoke: Palgrave Macmillan.

Thompson, S. and Thompson, N. (2008) *The Critically Reflective Practitioner*, Basingstoke: Palgrave Macmillan.

Vygotsky, L. S. (1978). *Mind in Society*, Cambridge, MA: Harvard College.

Wood, D. (1998) *How Children Think and Learn*, 2nd edn, Oxford: Blackwell.

Index